INTRODUCTION

When was the last time you read through the entire Bible? Have you ever read it cover to cover with others? Over the years we have come to believe that reading the Scriptures and growing in our faith are individual exercises. It is personal. However, the Scriptures are intended to be read in community. Traditionally a rabbi, or other community leader, would stand up, read from the Torah, and then a lively discussion would ensue. In this way, faith becomes a community endeavor with the Scriptures at its center. Our desire is to embody this way of living as a community of faith.

Beginning on Ash Wednesday of this year, 2020, we will set out, as a community of faith, to read the Bible in its entirety. We will start with the Gospel of Matthew. When we reach Easter we will have read all four of the gospels' accounts of the birth, life, suffering, death, and resurrection of Jesus. We will then continue reading the New Testament finishing with the Book of Revelation by June 11th. After that we will return to the beginning, Genesis.

We will continue reading the Old Testament and by Advent we will be deep into the Book of Job. We will end this year and kick-off the next reading the Psalms. Lent of 2021 will begin in Jeremiah and we will finish our reading by Easter. Over the course of 403 days, beginning on Ash Wednesday this year and finishing the day before Easter next year, we will complete the entire Bible together.

Throughout Lent and Advent, in addition to our daily readings, there will be an accompanying devotion. During these liturgical seasons our sermons will also align with our reading so that as a community we can dive a bit deeper, taking time to reflect on the Scriptures in light of the seasons.

I pray that you enjoy this time reading the Scriptures together with family and friends. And I trust that God will bless us, grow us in our faith, and lead us in our loving witness to this world.

Your Friend,
Jeff

READING SCHEDULE

LENT
Ash Wednesday, February 26 - Easter Sunday, April 12

- Day 1: (Ash) Wednesday, February 26 - Matthew chapters 1-2
- Day 2: Thursday, February 27 - Matthew chapters 3-4
- Day 3: Friday, February 28 - Matthew chapters 5-6
- Day 4: Saturday, February 29 - Matthew chapters 7-8

- Day 5: Sunday, March 1 - Matthew chapters 9-10
- Day 6: Monday, March 2 - Matthew chapters 11-12
- Day 7: Tuesday, March 3 - Matthew chapters 13-14
- Day 8: Wednesday, March 4 - Matthew chapters 15-16
- Day 9: Thursday, March 5 - Matthew chapters 17-18
- Day 10: Friday, March 6 - Matthew chapters 19-20
- Day 11: Saturday, March 7 - Matthew chapters 21-22

- Day 12: Sunday, March 8 - Matthew chapters 23-24
- Day 13: Monday, March 9 - Matthew chapters 25-26
- Day 14: Tuesday, March 10 - Matthew chapters 27-28
- Day 15: Wednesday, March 11 - Mark chapters 1-2
- Day 16: Thursday, March 12 - Mark chapters 3-4
- Day 17: Friday, March 13 - Mark chapters 5-6
- Day 18: Saturday, March 14 - Mark chapters 7-8

- Day 19: Sunday, March 15 - Mark chapters 9-10
- Day 20: Monday, March 16 - Mark chapters 11-12
- Day 21: Tuesday, March 17 - Mark chapters 13-14
- Day 22: Wednesday, March 18 - Mark chapters 15-16
- Day 23: Thursday, March 19 - Luke chapters 1-2
- Day 24: Friday, March 20 - Luke chapters 3-4
- Day 25: Saturday, March 21 - Luke chapters 5-6

- Day 26: Sunday, March 22 - Luke chapters 7-8
- Day 27: Monday, March 23 - Luke chapters 9-10
- Day 28: Tuesday, March 24 - Luke chapters 11-12
- Day 29: Wednesday, March 25 - Luke chapters 13-14
- Day 30: Thursday, March 26 - Luke chapters 15-16
- Day 31: Friday, March 27 - Luke chapters 17-18
- Day 32: Saturday, March 28 - Luke chapters 19-20

- Day 33: Sunday, March 29- Luke chapters 21-22
- Day 34: Monday, March 30 - Luke chapters 23-24
- Day 35: Tuesday, March 31 - John chapters 1-2
- Day 36: Wednesday, April 1 - John chapters 3-4
- Day 37: Thursday, April 2 - John chapters 5-6
- Day 38: Friday, April 3 - John chapters 7-8
- Day 39: Saturday, April 4 - John chapters 9-10

Holy Week
- Day 40: (Palm) Sunday, April 5 - John chapters 11-12
- Day 41: Monday, April 6 - John chapters 13-14
- Day 42: Tuesday, April 7 - John chapters 15-16
- Day 43: Wednesday, April 8 - John chapter 17
- Day 44: (Maundy) Thursday, April 9 - John chapter 18
- Day 45: (Good) Friday, April 10 - John chapter 19
- Day 46: Saturday, April 11 - John chapter 20

- Day 47: (Easter) Sunday, April 12 - John chapter 21

Monday, April 13 - Saturday, May 30
- Day 48: Monday, April 13 - Acts chapters 1-3
- Day 49: Tuesday, April 14 - Acts chapters 4-6
- Day 50: Wednesday, April 15 - Acts chapters 7-8
- Day 51: Thursday, April 16 - Acts chapters 9-10
- Day 52: Friday, April 17 - Acts chapters 11-13
- Day 53: Saturday, April 18 - Acts chapters 14-15

- Day 54: Sunday, April 19 - Acts chapters 16-17
- Day 55: Monday, April 20 - Acts chapters 18-20
- Day 56: Tuesday, April 21 - Acts chapters 21-23
- Day 57: Wednesday, April 22 - Acts chapters 24-26
- Day 58: Thursday, April 23 - Acts chapters 27-28
- Day 59: Friday, April 24 - Romans chapters 1-3
- Day 60: Saturday, April 25 - Romans chapters 4-7

- Day 61: Sunday, April 26 - Romans chapters 8-10
- Day 62: Monday, April 27 - Romans chapters 11-13
- Day 63: Tuesday, April 28 - Romans chapters 14-16
- Day 64: Wednesday, April 29 - 1 Corinthians chapters 1-4
- Day 65: Thursday, April 30 - 1 Corinthians chapters 5-8
- Day 66: Friday, May 1 - 1 Corinthians chapters 9-11
- Day 67: Saturday, May 2 - 1 Corinthians chapters 12-14

- Day 68: Sunday, May 3 - 1 Corinthians chapters 15-16
- Day 69: Monday, May 4 - 2 Corinthians chapters 1-4
- Day 70: Tuesday, May 5 - 2 Corinthians chapters 5-9
- Day 71: Wednesday, May 6 - 2 Corinthians chapters 10-13
- Day 72: Thursday, May 7 - Galatians chapters 1-3
- Day 73: Friday, May 8 - Galatians chapters 4-6
- Day 74: Saturday, May 9 - Ephesians chapters 1-3

- Day 75: Sunday, May 10 - Ephesians chapters 4-6
- Day 76: Monday, May 11 - Philippians chapters 1-2
- Day 77: Tuesday, May 12 - Philippians chapters 3-4
- Day 78: Wednesday, May 13 - Colossians chapters 1-2

- Day 79: Thursday, May 14 - Colossians chapters 3-4
- Day 80: Friday, May 15 - 1 Thessalonians chapters 1-2
- Day 81: Saturday, May 16 - 1 Thessalonians chapters 3-5

- Day 82: Sunday, May 17 - 2 Thessalonians chapters 1-3

- Day 83: Monday, May 18 - 1 Timothy chapters 1-3
- Day 84: Tuesday, May 19 - 1 Timothy chapters 4-6
- Day 85: Wednesday, May 20 - 2 Timothy chapters 1-2
- Day 86: Thursday, May 21 - 2 Timothy chapters 3-4
- Day 87: Friday, May 22 - Titus
- Day 88: Saturday, May 23 - Philemon

- Day 89: Sunday, May 24 - Hebrews chapters 1-3
- Day 90: Monday, May 25 - Hebrews chapters 4-6
- Day 91: Tuesday, May 26 - Hebrews chapters 7-9
- Day 92: Wednesday, May 27 - Hebrews chapters 10-11
- Day 93: Thursday, May 28 - Hebrews chapters 12-13
- Day 94: Friday, May 29 - James chapters 1-3
- Day 95: Saturday, May 30 - James chapters 4-5

Sunday, May 31 - Saturday, November 28
- Day 96: (Pentecost) Sunday, May 31 - 1 Peter chapters 1-3
- Day 97: Monday, June 1 - 1 Peter chapters 4-5
- Day 98: Tuesday, June 2 - 2 Peter chapters 1-3
- Day 99: Wednesday, June 3 - 1 John chapters 1-3
- Day 100: Thursday, June 4 - 1 John chapters 4-5
- Day 101: Friday, June 5 - 2 John
- Day 102: Saturday, June 6 - Jude

- Day 103: Sunday, June 7 - Revelation chapters 1-3
- Day 104: Monday, June 8 - Revelation chapters 4-8
- Day 105: Tuesday, June 9 - Revelation chapters 9-12
- Day 106: Wednesday, June 10 - Revelation chapters 13-16
- Day 107: Thursday, June 11 - Revelation chapters 17-19
- Day 108: Friday, June 12 - Revelation chapters 20-22
- Day 109: Saturday, June 13 - Genesis chapters 1-3

- Day 110: Sunday, June 14 - Genesis chapters 4-7
- Day 111: Monday, June 15 - Genesis chapters 8-11

- Day 112: Tuesday, June 16 - Genesis chapters 12-15
- Day 113: Wednesday, June 17 - Genesis chapters 16-18
- Day 114: Thursday, June 18 - Genesis chapters 19-21
- Day 115: Friday, June 19 - Genesis chapters 22-24
- Day 116: Saturday, June 20 - Genesis chapters 25-26

- Day 117: Sunday, June 21 - Genesis chapters 27-29
- Day 118: Monday, June 22 - Genesis chapters 30-31
- Day 119: Tuesday, June 23 - Genesis chapters 32-34
- Day 120: Wednesday, June 24 - Genesis chapters 35-37
- Day 121: Thursday, June 25 - Genesis chapters 38-40
- Day 122: Friday, June 26 - Genesis chapters 41-42
- Day 123: Saturday, June 27 - Genesis chapters 43-45

- Day 124: Sunday, June 28 - Genesis chapters 46-47
- Day 125: Monday, June 29 - Genesis chapters 48-50
- Day 126: Tuesday, June 30 - Exodus chapters 1-3
- Day 127: Wednesday, July 1 - Exodus chapters 4-6
- Day 128: Thursday, July 2 - Exodus chapters 7-9
- Day 129: Friday, July 3 - Exodus chapters 10-12
- Day 130: Saturday, July 4 - Exodus chapters 13-15

- Day 131: Sunday, July 5 - Exodus chapters 16-18
- Day 132: Monday, July 6 - Exodus chapters 19-21
- Day 133: Tuesday, July 7 - Exodus chapters 22-24
- Day 134: Wednesday, July 8 - Exodus chapters 25-27
- Day 135: Thursday, July 9 - Exodus chapters 28-29
- Day 136: Friday, July 10 - Exodus chapters 30-32
- Day 137: Saturday, July 11 - Exodus chapters 33-35

- Day 138: Sunday, July 12 - Exodus chapters 36-38
- Day 139: Monday, July 13 - Exodus chapters 39-40
- Day 140: Tuesday, July 14 - Leviticus chapters 1-4
- Day 141: Wednesday, July 15 - Leviticus chapters 5-7

- Day 142: Thursday, July 16 - Leviticus chapters 8-10
- Day 143: Friday, July 17 - Leviticus chapters 11-13
- Day 144: Saturday, July 18 - Leviticus chapters 14-15

- Day 145: Sunday, July 19 - Leviticus chapters 16-18
- Day 146: Monday, July 20 - Leviticus chapters 19-21
- Day 147: Tuesday, July 21 - Leviticus chapters 22-23
- Day 148: Wednesday, July 22 - Leviticus chapters 24-25
- Day 149: Thursday, July 23 - Leviticus chapters 26-27
- Day 150: Friday, July 24 - Numbers chapters 1-2
- Day 151: Saturday, July 25 - Numbers chapters 3-4

- Day 152: Sunday, July 26 - Numbers chapters 5-6
- Day 153: Monday, July 27 - Numbers chapter 7
- Day 154: Tuesday, July 28 - Numbers chapters 8-10
- Day 155: Wednesday, July 29 - Numbers chapters 11-13
- Day 156: Thursday, July 30 - Numbers chapters 14-15
- Day 157: Friday, July 31 - Numbers chapters 16-17
- Day 158: Saturday, August 1 - Numbers chapters 18-20

- Day 159: Sunday, August 2 - Numbers chapters 21-22
- Day 160: Monday, August 3 - Numbers chapters 23-25
- Day 161: Tuesday, August 4 - Numbers chapters 26-27
- Day 162: Wednesday, August 5 - Numbers chapters 28-30
- Day 163: Thursday, August 6 - Numbers chapters 31-32
- Day 164: Friday, August 7 - Numbers chapters 33-34
- Day 165: Saturday, August 8 - Numbers chapters 35-36

- Day 166: Sunday, August 9 - Deuteronomy chapters 1-2
- Day 167: Monday, August 10 - Deuteronomy chapters 3-4
- Day 168: Tuesday, August 11 - Deuteronomy chapters 5-6
- Day 169: Wednesday, August 12 - Deuteronomy chapters 7-8
- Day 170:Thursday, August 13 - Deuteronomy chapters 9-10

- Day 171: Friday, August 14 - Deuteronomy chapters 11-12
- Day 172: Saturday, August 15 - Deuteronomy chapters 13-14

- Day 173: Sunday, August 16 - Deuteronomy chapters 15-16
- Day 174: Monday, August 17 - Deuteronomy chapters 17-18
- Day 175: Tuesday, August 18 - Deuteronomy chapters 19-20
- Day 176: Wednesday, August 19 - Deuteronomy chapters 21-22
- Day 177: Thursday, August 20 - Deuteronomy chapters 23-24
- Day 178: Friday, August 21 - Deuteronomy chapters 25-26
- Day 179: Saturday, August 22 - Deuteronomy chapters 27-28

- Day 180: Sunday, August 23 - Deuteronomy chapters 29-30
- Day 181: Monday, August 24 - Deuteronomy chapters 31-32
- Day 182: Tuesday, August 25 - Deuteronomy chapters 33-34
- Day 183: Wednesday, August 26 - Joshua chapters 1-4
- Day 184: Thursday, August 27 - Joshua chapters 5-8
- Day 185: Friday, August 28 - Joshua chapters 9-11
- Day 186: Saturday, August 29 - Joshua chapters 12-15

- Day 187: Sunday, August 30 - Joshua chapters 16-18
- Day 188: Monday, August 31 - Joshua chapters 19-21
- Day 189: Tuesday, September 1 - Joshua chapters 22-24
- Day 190: Wednesday, September 2 - Judges chapters 1-2
- Day 191: Thursday, September 3 - Judges chapters 3-4
- Day 192: Friday, September 4 - Judges chapters 5-6
- Day 193: Saturday, September 5 - Judges chapters 7-8

- Day 194: Sunday, September 6 - Judges chapters 9-10
- Day 195: Monday, September 7 - Judges chapters 11-12
- Day 196: Tuesday, September 8 - Judges chapters 13-14
- Day 197: Wednesday, September 9 - Judges chapters 15-16
- Day 198: Thursday, September 10 - Judges chapters 17-18
- Day 199: Friday, September 11 - Judges chapters 19-1

- Day 200: Saturday, September 12 - Ruth chapters 1-2

- Day 201: Sunday, September 13 - Ruth chapters 3-4
- Day 202: Monday, September 14 - 1 Samuel chapters 1-3
- Day 203: Tuesday, September 15 - 1 Samuel chapters 4-8
- Day 204: Wednesday, September 16 - 1 Samuel chapters 9-12
- Day 205: Thursday, September 17 - 1 Samuel chapters 13-14
- Day 206: Friday, September 18 - 1 Samuel chapters 15-17
- Day 207: Saturday, September 19 - 1 Samuel chapters 18-20

- Day 208: Sunday, September 20 - 1 Samuel chapters 21-24
- Day 209: Monday, September 21 - 1 Samuel chapters 25-27
- Day 210: Tuesday, September 22 - 1 Samuel chapters 28-31
- Day 211: Wednesday, September 23 - 2 Samuel chapters 1-3
- Day 212: Thursday, September 24 - 2 Samuel chapters 4-7
- Day 213: Friday, September 25 - 2 Samuel chapters 8-12
- Day 214: Saturday, September 26 - 2 Samuel chapters 13-15

- Day 215: Sunday, September 27 - 2 Samuel chapters 16-18
- Day 216: Monday, September 28 - 2 Samuel chapters 19-21
- Day 217: Tuesday, September 29 - 2 Samuel chapters 22-24
- Day 218: Wednesday, September 30 - 1 Kings chapters 1-2
- Day 219: Thursday, October 1 - 1 Kings chapters 3-5
- Day 220: Friday, October 2 - 1 Kings chapters 6-7
- Day 221: Saturday, October 3 - 1 Kings chapters 8-9

- Day 222: Sunday, October 4 - 1 Kings chapters 10-11
- Day 223: Monday, October 5 - 1 Kings chapters 12-14
- Day 224: Tuesday, October 6 - 1 Kings chapters 15-17
- Day 225: Wednesday, October 7 - 1 Kings chapters 18-20
- Day 226: Thursday, October 8 - 1 Kings chapters 21-22
- Day 227: Friday, October 9 - 2 Kings chapters 1-3
- Day 228: Saturday, October 10 - 2 Kings chapters 4-5

- Day 229: Sunday, October 11 - 2 Kings chapters 6-8
- Day 230: Monday, October 12 - 2 Kings chapters 9-11
- Day 231: Tuesday, October 13 - 2 Kings chapters 12-14
- Day 232: Wednesday, October 14 - 2 Kings chapters 15-17
- Day 233: Thursday, October 15 - 2 Kings chapters 18-19
- Day 234: Friday, October 16 - 2 Kings chapters 20-22
- Day 235: Saturday, October 17 - 2 Kings chapters 23-25

- Day 236: Sunday, October 18 - 1 Chronicles chapters 1-2
- Day 237: Monday, October 19 - 1 Chronicles chapters 3-5
- Day 238: Tuesday, October 20 - 1 Chronicles chapter 6
- Day 239: Wednesday, October 21 - 1 Chronicles chapters 7-8
- Day 240: Thursday, October 22 - 1 Chronicles chapters 9-11
- Day 241: Friday, October 23 - 1 Chronicles chapters 12-14
- Day 242: Saturday, October 24 - 1 Chronicles chapters 15-17

- Day 243: Sunday, October 25 - 1 Chronicles chapters 18-21
- Day 244: Monday, October 26 - 1 Chronicles chapters 22-24
- Day 245: Tuesday, October 27 - 1 Chronicles chapters 25-27
- Day 246: Wed., October 28 - 1 Chronicles chapters 28-29
- Day 247: Thursday, October 29 - 2 Chronicles chapters 1-2
- Day 248: Friday, October 30 - 2 Chronicles chapters 3-4
- Day 249: Saturday, October 31 - 2 Chronicles chapters 5-6

- Day 250: Sunday, November 1 - 2 Chronicles chapters 7-8
- Day 251: Monday, November 2 - 2 Chronicles chapters 9-10
- Day 252: Tuesday, November 3 - 2 Chronicles chapters 11-12
- Day 253: Wed., November 4 - 2 Chronicles chapters 13-14
- Day 254: Thursday, November 5 - 2 Chronicles chapters 15-17
- Day 255: Friday, November 6 - 2 Chronicles chapters 18-20
- Day 256: Saturday, November 7 - 2 Chronicles chapters 21-22

- Day 257: Sunday, November 8 - 2 Chronicles chapters 23-24
- Day 258: Monday, November 9 - 2 Chronicles chapters 25-27

- Day 259: Tuesday, November 10 - 2 Chronicles chapters 28-29
- Day 260: Wed., November 11 - 2 Chronicles chapters 30-31
- Day 261: Thursday, November 12 - 2 Chronicles chapters 32-34
- Day 262: Friday, November 13 - 2 Chronicles chapters 35-36
- Day 263: Saturday, November 14 - Ezra chapters 1-3

- Day 264: Sunday, November 15 - Ezra chapters 4-7
- Day 265: Monday, November 16 - Ezra chapters 8-10
- Day 266: Tuesday, November 17 - Nehemiah chapters 1-3
- Day 267: Wednesday, November 18 - Nehemiah chapters 4-6
- Day 268: Thursday, November 19 - Nehemiah chapter 7
- Day 269: Friday, November 20 - Nehemiah chapters 8-9
- Day 270: Saturday, November 21 - Nehemiah chapters 10-11

- Day 271: Sunday, November 22 - Nehemiah chapters 12-13
- Day 272: Monday, November 23 - Esther chapters 1-5
- Day 273: Tuesday, November 24 - Esther chapters 6-10
- Day 274: Wednesday, November 25 - Job chapters 1-4
- Day 275: Thursday, November 26 - Job chapters 5-7
- Day 276: Friday, November 27 - Job chapters 8-10
- Day 277: Saturday, November 28 - Job chapters 11-13

ADVENT
Sunday, November 29 - Friday, December 25
- Day 278: First Sunday of Advent, Nov. 29 - Job chapters 14-16
- Day 279: Monday, November 30 - Job chapters 17-20
- Day 280: Tuesday, December 1 - Job chapters 21-23
- Day 281: Wednesday, December 2 - Job chapters 24-28
- Day 282: Thursday, December 3 - Job chapters 29-31
- Day 283: Friday, December 4 - Job chapters 32-34
- Day 284: Saturday, December 5 - Job chapters 35-37

- Day 285: Second Sunday of Advent, Dec. 6 - Job chpts. 38-39

- Day 286: Monday, December 7 - Job chapters 40-42
- Day 287: Tuesday, December 8 - Psalms 1-8
- Day 288: Wednesday, December 9 - Psalms 9-16
- Day 289: Thursday, December 10 - Psalms 17-20
- Day 290: Friday, December 11 - Psalms 21-25
- Day 291: Saturday, December 12 - Psalms 26-31

- Day 292: Third Sunday of Advent, Dec. 13 - Psalms 32-35
- Day 293: Monday, December 14 - Psalms 36-39
- Day 294: Tuesday, December 15 - Psalms 40-45
- Day 295: Wednesday, December 16 - Psalms 46-50
- Day 296: Thursday, December 17 - Psalms 51-57
- Day 297: Friday, December 18 - Psalms 58-65
- Day 298: Saturday, December 19 - Psalms 66-69

- Day 299: Fourth Sunday of Advent, Dec. 20 - Psalms 70-73
- Day 300: Monday, December 21 - Psalms 74-77
- Day 301: Tuesday, December 22 - Psalms 78-79
- Day 302: Wednesday, December 23 - Psalms 80-85
- Day 303: (Christmas Eve) Thursday, Dec. 24 - Psalms 86-89
- Day 304: (Christmas Day) Friday, December 25 - Psalms 90-95

Saturday, December 26 - Tuesday, February 16
- Day 305: Saturday, December 26 - Psalms 96-102

- Day 306: Sunday, December 27 - Psalms 103-105
- Day 307: Monday, December 28 - Psalms 106-107
- Day 308: Tuesday, December 29 - Psalms 108-114
- Day 309: Wednesday, December 30 - Psalms 115-118
- Day 310: Thursday, December 31 - Psalm 119:1-88
- Day 311: Friday, January 1 - Psalm 119:89-176
- Day 312: Saturday, January 2 - Psalms 120-132

- Day 313: Sunday, January 3 - Psalms 133-139

- Day 314: Monday, January 4 - Psalms 140-145
- Day 315: Tuesday, January 5 - Psalms 146-150
- Day 316: Wednesday, January 6 - Proverbs chapters 1-3
- Day 317: Thursday, January 7 - Proverbs chapters 4-6
- Day 318: Friday, January 8 - Proverbs chapters 7-9
- Day 319: Saturday, January 9 - Proverbs chapters 10-12

- Day 320: Sunday, January 10 - Proverbs chapters 13-15
- Day 321: Monday, January 11 - Proverbs chapters 16-18
- Day 322: Tuesday, January 12 - Proverbs chapters 19-21
- Day 323: Wednesday, January 13 - Proverbs chapters 22-23
- Day 324: Thursday, January 14 - Proverbs chapters 24-26
- Day 325: Friday, January 15 - Proverbs chapters 27-29
- Day 326: Saturday, January 16 - Proverbs chapters 30-31

- Day 327: Sunday, January 17 - Ecclesiastes chapters 1-4
- Day 328: Monday, January 18 - Ecclesiastes chapters 5-8
- Day 329: Tuesday, January 19 - Ecclesiastes chapters 9-12
- Day 330: Wed., January 20 - Song of Solomon chapters 1-4
- Day 331: Thursday, January 21 - Song of Solomon chapters 5-8
- Day 332: Friday, January 22 - Isaiah chapters 1-4
- Day 333: Saturday, January 23 - Isaiah chapters 5-8

- Day 334: Sunday, January 24 - Isaiah chapters 9-12
- Day 335: Monday, January 25 - Isaiah chapters 13-17
- Day 336: Tuesday, January 26 - Isaiah chapters 18-22
- Day 337: Wednesday, January 27 - Isaiah chapters 23-27
- Day 338: Thursday, January 28 - Isaiah chapters 28-30
- Day 339: Friday, January 29 - Isaiah chapters 31-35
- Day 340: Saturday, January 30 - Isaiah chapters 36-41

- Day 341: Sunday, January 31 - Isaiah chapters 42-44
- Day 342: Monday, February 1 - Isaiah chapters 45-48

- Day 343: Tuesday, February 2 - Isaiah chapters 49-53
- Day 344: Wednesday, February 3 - Isaiah chapters 54-58
- Day 345: Thursday, February 4 - Isaiah chapters 59-63
- Day 346: Friday, February 5 - Isaiah chapters 64-66
- Day 347: Saturday, February 6 - Jeremiah chapters 1-3

- Day 348: Sunday, February 7 - Jeremiah chapters 4-6
- Day 349: Monday, February 8 - Jeremiah chapters 7-9
- Day 350: Tuesday, February 9 - Jeremiah chapters 10-13
- Day 351: Wednesday, February 10 - Jeremiah chapters 14-17
- Day 352: Thursday, February 11 - Jeremiah chapters 18-22
- Day 353: Friday, February 12 - Jeremiah chapters 23-25
- Day 354: Saturday, February 13 - Jeremiah chapters 26-29

- Day 355: Sunday, February 14 - Jeremiah chapters 30-31
- Day 356: Monday, February 15 - Jeremiah chapters 32-34
- Day 357: Tuesday, February 16 - Jeremiah chapters 35-37

LENT
Wednesday, February 17 - Saturday, April 3
- Day 358: (Ash) Wednesday, Feb. 17 - Jeremiah chapters 38-41
- Day 359: Thursday, February 18 - Jeremiah chapters 42-45
- Day 360: Friday, February 19 - Jeremiah chapters 46-48
- Day 361: Saturday, February 20 - Jeremiah chapters 49-50

- Day 362: Sunday, February 21 - Jeremiah chapters 51-52
- Day 363: Monday, February 22 - Lamentations chapters 1:3:36
- Day 364: Tuesday, February 23 - Lamentations chapters 3:37-5
- Day 365: Wednesday, February 24 - Ezekiel chapters 1-4
- Day 366: Thursday, February 25 - Ezekiel chapters 5-8

- Day 367: Friday, February 26 - Ezekiel chapters 9-12
- Day 368: Saturday, February 27 - Ezekiel chapters 13-15

- Day 369: Sunday, February 28 - Ezekiel chapters 16-17
- Day 370: Monday, March 1 - Ezekiel chapters 18-20
- Day 371: Tuesday, March 2 - Ezekiel chapters 21-22
- Day 372: Wednesday, March 3 - Ezekiel chapters 23-24
- Day 373: Thursday, March 4 - Ezekiel chapters 25-27
- Day 374: Friday, March 5 - Ezekiel chapters 28-30
- Day 375: Saturday, March 6 - Ezekiel chapters 31-33

- Day 376: Sunday, March 7 - Ezekiel chapters 34-36
- Day 377: Monday, March 8 - Ezekiel chapters 37-39
- Day 378: Tuesday, March 9 - Ezekiel chapters 40-42
- Day 379: Wednesday, March 10 - Ezekiel chapters 43-45
- Day 380: Thursday, March 11 - Ezekiel chapters 46-48
- Day 381: Friday, March 12 - Daniel chapters 1-3
- Day 382: Saturday, March 13 - Daniel chapters 4-6

- Day 383: Sunday, March 14 - Daniel chapters 7-9
- Day 384: Monday, March 15 - Daniel chapters 10-12
- Day 385: Tuesday, March 16 - Hosea chapters 1-4
- Day 386: Wednesday, March 17 - Hosea chapters 5-7
- Day 387: Thursday, March 18 - Hosea chapters 8-11
- Day 388: Friday, March 19 - Hosea chapters 12-14
- Day 389: Saturday, March 20 - Joel

- Day 390: Sunday, March 21 - Amos chapters 1-5
- Day 391: Monday, March 22 - Amos chapters 6-9
- Day 392: Tuesday, March 23 - Obadiah
- Day 393: Wednesday, March 24 - Jonah
- Day 394: Thursday, March 25 - Micah chapters 1-3
- Day 395: Friday, March 26 - Micah chapters 4-7
- Day 396: Saturday, March 27 - Nahum

Holy Week

- Day 397: (Palm) Sunday, March 28 - Habakkuk
- Day 398: Monday, March 29 - Zephaniah
- Day 399: Tuesday, March 30 - Haggai
- Day 400: Wednesday, March 31 - Zechariah chapters 1-5
- Day 401: Thursday, April 1 - Zechariah chapters 6-10
- Day 402: (Good) Friday, April 2 - Zechariah chapters 11-14
- Day 403: Saturday, April 3 - Malachi

LENT 2020

Wednesday, February 26 - Saturday, April 11

Note: Much of the commentary found in the following daily devotions comes from John H. Sailhamer's, *NIV Compact Bible Commentary* (Grand Rapids, MI.: Zondervan Publishing House, 1994). Additional commentary comes from *The New Interpreter's Bible: A Commentary in Twelve Volumes* (Nashville, TN.: Abingdon Press, 1995)

2020 LENTEN READER
Ash Wednesday, February 26

Redemption

Today's Scripture Readings: Matthew chapters 1-2

"So he got up, took the child and his mother during the night and left for Egypt, where he stayed until the death of Herod. And so was fulfilled what the Lord had said through the prophet: 'Out of Egypt I called my son.'" (Matthew 2:14-15)

In this Gospel account, Matthew shares a story that shows God's protection of a young Jesus during his early years. Like Israel in the OT, Jesus had traveled to Egypt. When he with his family, came up out of Egypt, the author saw the hand of God not only protecting him from Herod's attempt to murder him, but also in fulfilling the words of the prophet Hosea: "Out of Egypt I called my son" (Hosea 11:1). Matthew saw in Israel's exodus from Egypt a picture of God's future redemption.

Herod's brutal order to "kill all the boys of Bethlehem and its vicinity who were two years old and under" parallels the order of Pharaoh, "Every boy that is born, you must throw into the Nile (Exodus 1:22). The similarity is not lost on Matthew. By the events of this story in his early life, Jesus is cast into the role of a new Moses, prepared in Egypt to lead his people into the Promised Land and to fulfill the blessings of Abraham.

From the onset of his Gospel, Matthew wants the reader to understand God brings redemption to those who follow Jesus in the same way God brought redemption to those who followed Moses.

Reflection:
As we begin Lent, take some time to ponder the question, "How have I experienced redemption from God by following Jesus?"

Prayer:
Dear Lord, please help me be aware of the ways in which you save me daily. Give me the wisdom to seek ways I need to continue to be saved. Give me the strength and courage to hand myself over to your salvation. Amen.

Thursday, February 27

Repentance

Today's Scripture Readings: Matthew chapters 3-4

"Produce fruit in keeping with repentance." (Matthew 3:8)

The beginning of Jesus' ministry is marked by the appearance of John the Baptist, preaching a message that the kingdom of heaven was near. He called upon Israel to repent in preparation for it. Matthew stresses the fact that there was a great response in Jerusalem and Judea to John's preaching. The response was so great even the Pharisees and Sadducees were responding (v.7). However, at their arrival John warns them with a challenge to "produce fruit in keeping with repentance."

Repentance is a word we do not often use in our culture today. It carries religious baggage and is often associated with other words like sin and confession; in other words, we don't really like to use "repentance" unless we are talking in church about someone else's need to "confess their sins and repent." When we do speak of repentance it is synonymous with apologizing and asking for forgiveness. That may be part of it but there is more; repentance requires change.

When our children tell us they are sorry, my wife and I have gotten in the habit of telling them, "then don't do it again." This is what John is telling the Pharisees and the Sadducees. It is not enough to just be sorry, or in this case, seek "shelter from the coming wrath." To truly repent we must not only recognize the error of our ways, we must also be willing to start living, speaking, and acting . . . differently. We must start living in ways that produce fruit in keeping with repentance.

Reflection:
Take some time today and consider what may need to change in your life as you follow Christ?

Prayer:
O God, help me to begin living in ways that produce fruit in keeping with repentance. Give me the courage to surrender my will to you so that your ways can become mine. Replace my heart with your heart so that your concerns become my concerns. Amen.

Friday, February 28

Humility

Today's Scripture Readings: Matthew chapters 5-6

"Beware of practicing your acts of righteousness before others in order to be seen by them; for then you have no reward from your Father in heaven." (Matthew 6:1)

Jesus begins his sermon with the Old Testament theme of "blessing." The focus of his teaching is the future kingdom. This kingdom is one for which its people must suffer presently, but who will find great reward later.

It is in light of the concept of waiting for the arrival of the kingdom that Jesus teaches his disciples how to live in God's blessing and joy. Such a life, Jesus says, should serve as a beacon to the world, giving glory to God. It is a life that does not abolish the Scriptures, but rather fulfills God's intentions in giving his word to Israel. This life calls for a righteousness that goes beyond that of the scribes and the Pharisees.

The standard of righteousness that Jesus appeals to in this sermon is not that of human wisdom or traditional values. Jesus states clearly at the conclusion of this section of his sermon that citizens of the kingdom of God are to "be perfect, therefore, as God is perfect." With the call of righteousness comes the warning of self-righteousness and hypocrisy. The central theme of the second half of the sermon is service to God, "who sees what is done in secret," rather than service before other people. In the midst of these repeated warnings against hypocrisy, Jesus calls for an absolute trust in God and commitment to God's kingdom.

Reflection:
As you go about your day, are you able to identify ways you struggle with your own pride?

Prayer:
In my attempt to live in a way that brings you glory and honor, help me not to begin to take pride in the way I live. Help me to remain humble and not to stumble into the trap of arrogance and self-righteousness. Guard my heart so I do not seek the praise of others and in the process become a hypocrite slandering the kingdom of God. Amen.

Saturday, February 29

Testimony

Today's Scripture Readings: Matthew chapters 7-8

"Then Jesus said to him, 'See that you don't tell anyone. But go, show yourself to the priest and offer the gift Moses commanded, as a testimony to them.'" (Matthew 8:4)

Beginning in Chapter 8, Matthew records several incidents in Jesus' ministry that focus on the recognition of his authority among the people and the Jewish leaders. These are not random incidents, however. The specific examples of Jesus' acts recorded here correspond to the list of proof offered to the imprisoned John the Baptist in Chapter 11.

In the account of the healing of the leper, the man says simply, "Lord, if you are willing, you can make me clean." There is no question of Jesus' ability to heal. All depends on his sovereign will. Jesus replied, "I am willing, be clean!" to show that Jesus' teaching did not abolish the Law of Moses, Matthew adds Jesus' instruction to the leper that he now show himself to the priest, "and offer the gift Moses commanded." It may be significant, however, that the purpose of obeying what Moses commanded was to be "a testimony to them."

It is Christ's will that we would all be healed. Furthermore, our healing, and faithful response, become an opportunity for testimony.

Reflection:
How have you faithfully responded and used your story of healing as a testimony?

Prayer:
Dear Lord, thank you for the ways in which you have healed me. Provide me with opportunities to share my story of healing with others. Give me the strength and courage to share my story. And through the sharing of my story may I glorify your son. Amen.

Sunday, March 1

Acts of Mercy

Today's Scripture Readings: Matthew chapters 9-10

"As you go, proclaim this message: 'The kingdom of heaven has come near.' Heal the sick, raise the dead, cleanse those who have leprosy, drive out demons. Freely you have received; freely give." (Matthew 10:7-8)

At the beginning of chapter 10, Matthew states that Jesus" gave [the disciples] authority to drive out evil spirits and to heal every disease and sickness." In this way, the same divine authority that the preceding stories demonstrated as operative in the life of Jesus was not given to his disciples.

Jesus sent his disciples throughout the land of Israel to announce the coming of the messianic King. In Matthew's gospel this is the prelude to the people's rejection of this King. Matthew, however, records Jesus' instructions to his disciples in such a way that they provide a guide to the evangelistic mission of his own readers in the early church.

As readers of Matthew's gospel we also receive Jesus' instructions. Matthew intended for this to be a manual, of sorts, for evangelism and discipleship. In verses 7-8 Jesus gives the disciples two tasks: 1) share the story; and 2) engage in acts of mercy. We are *not* asked to *either* share the story *or* engage in acts of mercy, these go hand in hand. The good works are our opportunity to live in the story.

Reflection:
On this first Sunday of Lent take time to consider how you share the story of Jesus and demonstrate Christ's grace through acts of mercy. Are you engaged in both?

Prayer:
Dear Lord, please provide me opportunities this week to show the love of God through acts of mercy and then give me the courage to explain the story I am living. Amen.

Monday, March 2

Christ's Kin

Today's Scripture Readings: Matthew chapters 11-12

"Whoever does the will of my Father in heaven is my brother and sister and mother." (Matthew 12:50)

At this point in this gospel, the attention turns away from the present establishment of the kingdom of God to its rejection by Israel. Whether one speaks of a "postponement" of this kingdom or of a mere inauguration of the kingdom with a delayed consummation, the fact remains that a shift takes place here that ultimately leads to the establishment of the church and the opening of the Gospel to all nations.

The rejection of Jesus by the leaders of Israel is shown in chapter 12. They first accuse Jesus and his disciples of breaking the Law of Moses. Jesus responds: "It is lawful to do good on the Sabbath." Then the Pharisees attribute Jesus' works to the work of Beelzebub. Jesus responds to them not only by pointing out the desperate absurdity of their charge, but also by cautioning them of the seriousness of their rejection of God's offer: "by your words you will be acquitted, and by your words you will be condemned." In these stern words to the Pharisees, Matthew may also be warning his readers of the seriousness of rejecting Jesus offer: "Come to me, all you who are weary and burdened, and I will give you rest . . . and you will find rest for your souls."

Reflection:

Jesus is claiming authority over the Mosaic Law and going so far as to say acts of mercy surpass, or perhaps fulfill the law. This is the will of the Father. At the end of this section, Jesus claims that the ones who engage in acts of mercy are the ones who are his brother, sister, and mother. We run the risk of rejecting God's Kingdom when we cling too tightly to the law. Spend some time today reflecting on your relationship with Christ.

Prayer:

Hello God. Help me understand what it means to call you Father. Stretch my heart this day. Allow me to grow in grace and mercy. Forgive me when I reject the offer to find rest. Amen.

Tuesday, March 3

See It

Today's Scripture Readings: Matthew chapters 13-14

"For truly I tell you, many prophets and righteous people longed to see what you see but did not see it, and to hear what you hear but did not hear it." (Matthew 13:17)

Many years ago, while I was still in high school, my mother had gotten up in the middle of the night to get a drink from the kitchen. As she was walking through the house in the dark she noticed my dad has also gotten up. She watched him as he made his way past her also heading toward the kitchen. She spoke his name and he jumped in surprise. When she asked him how he had managed to walk right by without seeing her, he responded, "I wasn't looking for you."

The kingdom that Jesus offered to all those who would accept it is now illustrated in seven parables: the sower, the weeds, the mustard seed, the yeast, the hidden treasure, the pearl, and the net. Though each parable makes its own contribution to the reader's understanding of the kingdom, each also expresses the same basic truth. Jesus came to establish the kingdom promised in the OT prophetic literature, and he was, in fact, about to fulfill his mission. That kingdom, however - which was to be a visible, universal rule of the Messiah - would begin in a small, almost imperceptible, form, as a mustard seed or as a piece of yeast in a lump of dough. Unlike what might have been anticipated from reading the OT, there was to be a delay between the coming of the King and the consummation of the kingdom. During that delay, kingdom members were to live in expectation of the return of the King and the final establishment of the kingdom at the "end of the age."

Reflection:
As people who are living between the coming of the King and the consummation of the kingdom are we looking and listening for signs of the kingdom? Are we looking for the small acts of Christ in our world?

Prayer:
Father, help me to watch for the small, almost imperceptible, forms in which the kingdom presents itself. May I be able to help it grow. Amen.

Wednesday, March 4

A Clean Heart

Today's Scripture Readings: Matthew chapters 15-16

"These people honor me with their lips, but their hearts are far from me." (Matthew 15:8)

At the end of chapter 14 Jesus enters the area of Gennesaret. Matthew gives a short summary account of Jesus' activities there. The stress is on the fact that he healed many sick. Here also we are given a foretaste of the situation in Jerusalem. Jesus is met by Pharisees and teachers of the law who are scandalized by Jesus' disciples' apparent disregard for their "traditions." Jesus answers their accusations with his own exposition of the importance of the word of God over against tradition. What makes for purity and righteousness is not conformity to external rules and regulations, but rather a clean heart.

This argument of tradition and Scripture brings to mind the Wesleyan Quadrilateral: Scripture, Tradition, Experience, and Reason. Our faith and how we live it out is developed primarily by Scripture engaged through tradition, experience, and reason. When either tradition, experience or reason becomes more important than Scripture, or when we fail to use all three in our engagement with Scripture, we run the risk of our faith becoming rigid, focused on rules and regulations; or "pollyannaish," all comfort with no conviction. However, when we engage Scripture with tradition and reason and experience we open ourselves up to God creating in us a clean heart.

Reflection:
What is the primary force shaping your faith? Tradition? Experience? Reason? Scripture? Are you engaging Scripture to understand tradition, experience, and reason? Are you using tradition, experience and reason to understand Scripture? Are you using Scripture to defend your tradition, experience, or reason?

Prayer:
Dear Lord, search my heart. Go to the places I am afraid to go and find there the things I thought I had hidden. Pull them out and make in me a clean heart. Help me to honor you with the core of my being. Amen.

Thursday, March 5

Imagine the Possibilities

Today's Scripture Readings: Matthew chapters 17-18

"Truly I tell you, if you have faith as small as a mustard seed, you can say to this mountain, 'Move from here to there,' and it will move. Nothing will be impossible for you."
(Matthew 17:20b)

In the story of Jesus' healing the boy with a demon, a parallel between Jesus and Israel is drawn. Jesus says, "O unbelieving and perverse generation . . . how long shall I stay with you?" These words readily evoke the image of Israel's failure to believe God in the desert: "The LORD said to Moses, 'How long will these people treat me with contempt? How long will they refuse to believe in me, in spite of all the miraculous signs I have performed among them?'" (Numbers 14:11; cf. Psalm 95:10). Faith was the missing factor in Israel's relationship with God, and it could threaten to be the missing factor in the church. With faith, however, "nothing will be impossible."

I once heard a story of a prominent church leader from Korea visiting the United States. He was brought to all of our largest churches. He was shown all of our beautiful architecture and art work. He was given tours of historical sights where important events took place which shaped the faith of our country and gave rise to our denominations. At the end of his tour he was asked to share his thoughts. He replied, "It is amazing what you have been able to accomplish without the Holy Spirit."

Reflection:
Think about your faith. How much of your faith has been constructed by you for you? How much of your faith has been constructed by the Holy Spirit to change you? How much greater could it be?

Prayer:
Dear Lord, send your Holy Spirit into my heart this day so that I may surrender myself to your leading. Give me the courage to allow you to shape my faith and direct my life. Let me trust that what you have for me is greater than what I know. Let me find freedom in release. Amen.

Friday, March 6

Who Do You Trust

Today's Scripture Readings: Matthew chapters 19-20

" Jesus said to him, "If you wish to be perfect, go, sell your possessions, and give the money to the poor, and you will have treasure in heaven; then come, follow me.'" (Matthew 19:21)

Jesus' teaching regarding wealth was followed closely by the early church in Jerusalem. Jesus said, "If you want to be perfect, go, sell all your possessions and give to the poor." In the church in Acts, "all the believers were together and had everything in common. Selling their possessions and goods, they gave to anyone as they had need" (Acts 2:44-45).

This is not really about wealth or possessions, it is about trust. A person who has accumulated much finds it harder to trust than a person who has nothing. We even have a saying which reflects this truth: "What have you got to lose?" Though it is hard for a rich man to enter the kingdom of heaven, it is not impossible. Salvation does not depend on a person's wealth, or lack of it. The parable of the vineyard workers shows that salvation does not depend on the amount of work done, but on the generous grace of God. Those who put themselves first, however, "will be the last in the kingdom of heaven, and many who are last will be first."

Jesus himself set the supreme example of his teaching in willingly giving up his own life. Though his disciples may want to gain equal honor with Jesus in his kingdom, only Jesus knows the real price that must be paid, "to give his life as a ransom for many." The glorious and victorious Son of Man must first become the Suffering Servant. Only the blind will see him.

Reflection:
Do you trust God enough to let go? What do you need to let go of? What is your "treasured possession?" In what do you find your comfort and assurance? What do you trust with your life?

Prayer:
Hello God. Today help me learn to fully trust in you rather than my own strength, wealth, understanding, or position. Make me stand humbly before your Son. Amen.

Saturday, March 7

Repentance

Today's Scripture Readings: Matthew chapters 21-22

"The crowds that went ahead of him and that followed were shouting, 'Hosanna to the Son of David! Blessed is the one who comes in the name of the Lord! Hosanna in the highest heaven!'" (Matthew 21:9)

When Jesus arrived at Jerusalem, the crowds were ready, and he entered just as the prophets had foretold the Messiah would come: "See, your king comes to you, gentle and riding on a donkey." But when asked who Jesus was, they reveal their lingering lack of understanding: "This is Jesus, the prophet from Nazareth in Galilee." Their answer stands in sharp contrast to that of Peter's: "You are the Christ, the Son of the living God." The importance of this difference can be seen in the fact that the church is built on Peter's confession, whereas at the trial of Jesus a week later, this same crowd shouted "Crucify him!"

As had been promised in the OT, the Messiah would be recognized for his zeal for the house of God, the temple. The children welcomed Jesus as the "Son of David," but the chief priests "were indignant" and sought to undermine his authority. Jesus again looked to the work of John the Baptist as the one who announced his coming. The chief priests and the elders offered insincere repentance at the preaching of John and thus, in Jesus' parable, were like the son who agreed to work for his father but did not go out into the field. On the other hand, the true members of God's kingdom were those who repented at John's preaching like, "the tax collectors and the prostitutes." Repentance at John's preaching is that which led to faith in Jesus.

Reflection:
Many people repented upon hearing both John the Baptist and Jesus' preaching. Yet their reason for repentance was quite different and their expectations were not the same. What are your expectations? What is the point of repentance?

Prayer:
Hello Lord. Help me understand what I mean when I cry out to you: "Hosanna to the Son of David! Blessed is the one who comes in the name of the Lord! Hosanna in the highest heaven!" Amen.

Sunday, March 8

Humility

Today's Scripture Readings: Matthew chapters 23-24

"All who exalt themselves will be humbled and all who humble themselves will be exalted." (Matthew 23:12)

Taking the occasion of the attempts of the Pharisees to trap him in a matter of the law, Jesus turns to the crowd and his own disciples to condemn the hypocrisy of "the teachers of the law." He begins by acknowledging the legitimate office held by these teachers as interpreters of Mosaic Law: they "sit in Moses' seat." Thus what they teach, in so far as it is the teaching of Mosaic Law, must be obeyed by those under the Mosaic covenant. The problem does not lie in what they teach but in their own lack of obedience. They teach one thing and do another. As Jesus has repeatedly taught in this gospel, the teaching of the Law is directed to the heart. As for the teachers of the Law and the Pharisees, however, "everything they do is done for people to see." Jesus then drove home the point with a scathing series of seven "woes."

People judge us by our actions and our words. That is to say, people's opinions of us depend greatly on observed behavior. We are considered to be a person of character when our observable behaviors are consistent; when our words and our actions align. However, when what we say and what we do are out of sync we are deemed hypocrites. The misalignment often points to a deeper issue; a heart problem. On the other hand, God does not judge us by our actions but by our hearts; our motivations. Often, the only people we are fooling are ourselves.

Reflection:
We fall into the same trap as the Pharisees and religious teachers. In our effort to be faithful people of God we focus so much on our outward actions that we fail to guard our hearts and they grow hard toward others. How is my heart?

Prayer:
Dear Lord, as I go about my day today help me to focus on my heart toward others. Help me to engage people with compassion. Push me beyond my scope of friends and challenge me to grow. In your most holy and precious name I pray. Amen.

Monday, March 9

Betrayal

Today's Scripture Readings: Matthew chapters 25-26

"Truly I tell you, one of you will betray me." (Matthew 26:21b)

Matthew is careful to note that the death of Jesus happened at the time of the Jewish Passover. Thus two central themes from the OT are linked in Jesus' death: The Messianic Son of Man is identified as the Passover lamb. Matthew thus reflects the same understanding of the death of Christ as the apostle Paul, who wrote, "Christ, our Passover lamb, has been sacrificed." That Jesus was fully aware of his impending death is evident from his response to the woman "with an alabaster jar of very expensive perfume, which she poured on his head as he was reclining at the table." Jesus saw this as a preparation for his burial. At the same time, Judas Iscariot sought an opportunity to betray Jesus to the chief priests.

Jesus celebrated the Passover meal with his disciples on the evening he was betrayed. During the meal, he identified his own death with the bread and wine of the Passover meal. At the same time he identified his death as the fulfillment of a covenant "for many for the forgiveness of sins."

As Jesus and his disciples left the place of the meal and moved toward Gethsemane, Matthew, as the other gospels, stresses that Jesus was to face his death alone. He left his closest disciples and then, in the garden, he anticipated his separation even from the Father. Though Jesus was fully aware of what was about to happen to him in Jerusalem, the disciples were sleepy and tired of waiting, and they quickly fell asleep.

Reflection:
We all betray Jesus. Some of us, like Judas, do it for personal gain. Some of us, like Peter and the other disciples, do it out of fear or simply inattentiveness. How have you betrayed Jesus? Why?

Prayer:
Dear God, thank you for your forgiveness before, during, and after my moments of betrayal. Thank you for the faithfulness of your Son. Amen.

Tuesday, March 10

The Story

Today's Scripture Readings: Matthew chapters 27-28

"Go therefore and make disciples of all nations, baptizing them in the name of the Father and of the Son and of the Holy Spirit." (Matthew 28:19)

Matthew assures his readers that Jesus' tomb was secured, lest "his disciples come and steal the body and tell the people that he [had] been raised from the dead." Thus, when he writes of the Resurrection, there can be no talk of hoax. As the angel first announced the birth of Jesus to his mother, Mary, so now the angel announced his resurrection to the two Marys at the tomb. While the guards were being paid off to tell a different story, the women having seen Jesus on their way back to Jerusalem, were joyfully telling the disciples what they had seen.

Jesus, having met his disciples in Galilee, sent his disciples out to "make disciples of all nations," promising to be with them till the end of the age. Matthew's gospel has reached its climax, the end toward which it was heading - the good news was now to be proclaimed to Gentiles as well as to the Jews.

Reflection:
As Matthew's gospel comes to an end there is an attempt by some to change the story of Jesus to fit their own story. Do you

do this? Are you trying to live into Christ's story or are you trying to make Christ fit into your story? Whose story are you telling? Whose story are you living?

Prayer:
Dear Lord, please help me to surrender my attempts to make myself the star of the story. Help me to look for ways I can participate and live in your story; drawing others to you. Amen.

Wednesday, March 11

The Gospel

Today's Scripture Readings: Mark chapters 1-2

> *"The beginning of the good news of Jesus Christ,*
> *the Son of God" (Mark 1:1)*

Mark describes Jesus from the very start as the "Son of God." Is this verse a title of the book as a whole or only of the first section of Mark? The context suggests that Mark intended this first verse both as an introduction to the book and as a description of its first major section, the ministry of John the Baptist, which is, strictly speaking, "the beginning" of the gospel. It may be a part of Mark's larger purpose to fill out the content of the gospel to include it's "beginning" with John. This would have the effect of including, as well, the works of Christ during his earthly ministry as part of "the gospel."

"Gospel" simply means "good news." For some, the good news of Christ is to be found in the crucifixion. For others it is the resurrection. And for some, the good news is the arrival of the Holy Spirit. Yet, depending on how we read this simple verse, Mark could be claiming that the good news is the entire life of Christ; not just his death or resurrection.

Reflection:
How we understand the gospel determines how we live out our faith. What does the word "gospel" mean to you? How does that impact your faith? Your life?

Prayer:
Dear God, may I find good news for my life in the life of your Son, Jesus the Christ. Help me to strive to live as he lived and love as he loved. Amen.

Thursday, March 12

Out of His Mind

Today's Scripture Readings: Mark chapters 3-4

"When his family heard it, they went out to restrain him, for people were saying, 'He has gone out of his mind.'" (Mark 3:21)

Mark 3:2-35 gives an assessment of the judgments that were being formed about Jesus - by his kinsman and by the religious leaders in Jerusalem. The charge made by the teachers of the law from Jerusalem is stated in verse 22 - "He is possessed by Beelzebub! By the price of demons." Jesus demonstrates that such a charge was gravely dangerous and false. The parable is concluded with a stern warning that blasphemy against the Holy Spirit is unforgivable.

Mark, apparently sensing the severity of Jesus' words, adds the explanation in verse 30 that Jesus had warned the scribes in this instance because "they were saying, 'He has an unclean spirit.'" This passage has troubled many people throughout the history of the church and, given Mark's special attention to it, must have been a question already in his day: What is blasphemy against the Holy Spirit? The use of the verb tense here indicates that the sin of the scribes was not just the uttering of a sentence, but rather a "fixed attitude of mind." Both Matthew and Luke add, "Knowing their thoughts he said to them . . ."

Reflection:
The teachings of Jesus can be offensive and hard for us to hear, accept, and comprehend. When we find ourselves confronted and challenged by Christ we have the tendency to dismiss it or simply try to reason it away because we do not want to change our hearts. Where in your life have you been challenged by Christ? Where have you dismissed him?

Prayer:
Dear Lord, create in me a pure heart; a heart that desires nothing more than to be transformed by the Holy Spirit. Help me when I begin to dig in my heels. I pray this in your most holy and precious name. Amen.

Friday, March 13

I Know That Guy

Today's Scripture Readings: Mark chapters 5-6

"Isn't this the carpenter? Isn't this Mary's son and the brother of James, Joseph, Judas and Simon? Aren't his sisters here with us?" And they took offense at him." (Mark 6:3)

Mark concludes his narrative of the ministry of Jesus in Galilee by an account of his rejection in his own city. The words of the close friends of Jesus' family ("Isn't this Mary's son?") provide a striking contrast to Mark's overall presentation of Jesus as "the Son of God." Their question, which remains unanswered within this narrative, receives a resounding reply in the words of the centurion standing beneath the cross when Jesus died: "Surely this man was the Son of God" (15:39).

Jesus used a proverb to explain his rejection: "Only in his hometown, among his relatives and in his own house is a prophet without honor." Through this proverb, Mark gives further proof that Jesus' claims were true. His rejection in his own city prove he was a true prophet!

Reflection:

I have been married for 26 years. My wife and I rarely surprise one another anymore. It is not so bad that we can actually finish each other's sentences, but we often know what the other is going to say before they even speak. This story not only points to the validity of Jesus' claim, it also stands as a warning to us who claim to follow Christ. We need to be careful that we do not begin to feel as if we know Jesus so well that he has nothing left to teach us.

How are you trying to allow Jesus to speak to you again in fresh new ways?

Prayer:
Dear Lord, forgive me for those times when I stop listening because I don't think you have anything new left to tell me. Help me to lean into you as a person eager to learn and be transformed. Amen.

Saturday, March 14

The Blind Man

Today's Scripture Readings: Mark chapters 7-8

"They came to Bethsaida, and some people brought a blind man and begged Jesus to touch him." (Mark 8:22)

In Mark 8:1-26, the author has arranged several scenes to show the gradual process of Jesus' removing the blindness of those around him. First he recounts Jesus' feeding the four thousand. As with the earlier story of feeding the five thousand, Mark's emphasis falls on the similarity between Jesus' miracle and God's gift of manna to the Israelites in the desert. Mark also emphasizes that unlike the manna, the bread provided by Jesus can be "left over" for continual provision. It is, in fact, this very point that Jesus stresses to his disciples in the next section when they are again worried that they have no bread to eat. Mark's point is to show that unlike Moses in the desert, Jesus continuously provides over and above what they will need. This is what the disciples "still do not understand."

To show that such an understanding comes as a gradual process, Mark recounts the story of the healing of the blind man at Bethsaida. When this man was "healed," he could see but only partially. This man's sight provides the perfect picture of Mark's view of the disciples' faith. Only when Jesus touches him again he can see perfectly.

The growing faith of the disciples is contrasted with the permanent blindness of the Pharisees. They do not receive a sign from heaven because they come to test Jesus. Thus when the disciples fail to appreciate the significance of Jesus' providing bread for the four thousand and five thousand and begin to worry that they have no bread, Jesus warns them of the "yeast of the Pharisees and that of Harod." That yeast was their hardness of heart and failure to understand what they saw and heard.

Reflection:
What "blindness" can Jesus cure in you?

Prayer:
Dear God, by its very definition I am unable to see the blindness in myself. Give me the courage to acknowledge that I am blind and, in my heart, give me the desire to be healed and see. Amen.

Sunday, March 15

Faith and Understanding

Today's Scripture Readings: Mark chapters 9-10

> *"Immediately the boy's father exclaimed, 'I do believe; help me overcome my unbelief!'" (Mark 9:24)*

The story of the healing of the possessed boy turns on two different but related points. It first shows that faith is the key to God's work and power. When the disciples were unable to drive out the evil spirit, Jesus replied, "O unbelieving generation . . . how long shall I stay with you?" Then Jesus, turning further to the boy's father, said, "Everything is possible for him who believes." The father confessed, "I do believe," but then added, "Help me overcome my unbelief!" Thus without placing blame directly on either the disciples or the father, Jesus stressed the central importance of faith.

Faith must grow to maturity. Though an element of faith was present with the disciples and the father, it was not sufficient to cast out the evil spirit. Mark is here challenging his readers to go beyond an initial recognition of Jesus as the Son of God; they must strengthen their faith through prayer. What kind of prayer? The answer lies in the father's request, "Help me overcome my unbelief!" When the father asked for more faith, the son was healed.

The need for more faith is reinforced in the following segment, verses 30-32. Here Jesus again reminds the disciples of his impending betrayal and death. The disciples, however, "did not understand what he meant and were afraid to ask him about it." The readiness of the boy's father to ask Jesus for more faith is contrasted with the disciples' hesitance to ask Jesus for more understanding.

Reflection:
Mark teaches us that as followers of Christ we should not only be striving to grow in our faith but also in our understanding. We must guard against believing that our faith or our understanding is complete because this can lead to the delusion of self sufficiency. Are you still striving to grow in faith and understanding? How?

Prayer:
Dear Lord, please forgive my arrogance in those moments where I believe that my faith and my knowledge are sufficient. Help me find the humility to trust you and the courage to not rely on my own understanding. Amen.

Monday, March 16

Withered

Today's Scripture Readings: Mark chapters 11-12

"Seeing in the distance a fig tree in leaf, he went to find out if it had any fruit." (Mark 11:13a)

In 11:12-25, Mark tells the story of Jesus cleaning out the Temple upon his arrival in Jerusalem. As a way of interpreting Jesus' actions in the temple, Mark begins and ends the story with a fig tree.

The fig tree is cursed for not producing fruit. Mark adds the explanation that the figs were not in season - thus Jesus was cursing the tree, not simply because it had not produced fruit, but because it was a symbol of the unfaithfulness of the people of God.

Like the fig tree, the worship of the people at the temple was not pleasing to God. There was no faith there. Jesus drove out those who focused on the external aspects of Israel's worship. His actions were a warning of impending judgment on the people.

Reflection:
For many of us, we spend more time thinking about our actions than we do about our intentions. We are more concerned with what people think of us and the health of our reputation than we

are with the wellbeing of our souls. We want people to think we are nice but inside we are withered. A friend of mine recently told me, "Nice is not a fruit of the Spirit." How is it with your soul? Are you pretending?

Prayer:
God, let your peace be present in me and through me. Create in me a pure heart where my actions and my Spirit are aligned with you. May your concerns be my concerns; your joys my joys. Amen.

Tuesday, March 17

Abomination

Today's Scripture Readings: Mark chapters 13-14

"When you see 'the abomination that causes desolation' standing where it does not belong—let the reader understand—then let those who are in Judea flee to the mountains." (Mark 13:14)

Jesus now begins to describe what the "beginning" of the end will be like (vv.9-13). His description resembles some of the events that happened to the early Christians in the book of Acts: "You will be handed over to the local councils [Sahnedrins] and flogged in the synagogues" (v.9). But much of it goes far beyond those events, such as the event that Jesus describes in v.14, "'the abomination that causes desolation' standing where it does not belong."

What is the "abomination that causes desolation"? Mark himself inserts a comment to the reader at this point in the text, calling on him to take special note. Why? Because the "abomination that causes desolation" is specifically developed elsewhere in Scripture (Daniel 9:25-27), and he wants his readers to draw on that passage for understanding of this one. Mark thus presupposes a general knowledge of "the events of the end." His intent is not to restate such matters, but rather to provide the reader with Jesus' own warnings and admonitions about how his followers should live up to and during these days.

It is true that Christians through the ages have gained great strength and comfort from just these words of admonition. The world has never been without a time when much of what Jesus here speaks of was in evidence - e.g. wars and rumors of wars, earthquakes and famines (vv.7-8). Indeed, individual Christians and groups of all kinds have believed strongly that this or that series of events in their own day was the signal of the end of which Jesus here speaks. Nevertheless, at no time in history have all of these events come together in a way that permits one to say Jesus' words have already been fulfilled. They still await fulfillment.

Reflection:
What words of Jesus bring you comfort? To what promise of Christ do you cling?

Prayer:
Dear Lord, in your words help us find comfort. In your promises may we find admonition. Amen.

Wednesday, March 18

The End

Today's Scripture Readings: Mark chapters 15-16

*"Trembling and bewildered, the women went out and fled from
the tomb. They said nothing to anyone,
because they were afraid." (Mark 16:8)*

The main body of the gospel of Mark concludes with an account
of the resurrection of Jesus. Mark focuses only on the empty
tomb and the angel who announced to the women that Jesus had
risen from the dead. The angel told the women to tell the
disciples and Peter that they would see Jesus in Galilee, as he
had told them (14:28). The woman fled from the tomb "trembling
and bewildered" and, out of great fear, told no one what they had
seen and heard (16:8). The ending of Mark found in the NIV
(vv.9-20) is not attested by the earliest manuscripts. Most believe
it was attached to the end of the book at a much later date. It
summarizes the last events of Jesus' time on earth after the
Resurrection. Most of the material can be found in Matthew,
Luke, and Acts.

Reflection:
Mark intentionally left the end of his Gospel open. He did not feel
the need to wrap it up nice and neat. Rather, he left his first
readers wondering. Obviously the women told someone because
you know the story and believe today. Yet others, upon reading

Mark's account, felt the need to complete or even correct his telling of Christ's story. How comfortable are you with not knowing everything? Is there space in your faith to trust God with the story?

Prayer:
Dear Lord, please help me to find comfort in the midst of not knowing. Help me to see the small glimpses of your work in this life and let that be enough for me. Grant me the strength of character to trust in you even when the story doesn't go the way I think it should. Amen.

Thursday, March 19

The Lord has Done This For Me

Today's Scripture Readings: Luke chapters 1-2

> *"The Lord has done this for me," she said.*
> *"In these days he has shown his favor and taken away my*
> *disgrace among the people." (Luke 1:25)*

Luke begins with John the Baptist. However, he begins not with John himself, nor with his call to ministry, but with his family heritage and birth. As with the great prophets and patriarchs of the past, before his conception John's mother, Elizabeth, was barren. His birth was thus a miraculous sign that God was beginning to work among his people. There are numerous parallels between the birth of John and that of the prophet Samuel. For example, Samuel was the forerunner of King David, just as John was the forerunner of the Son of David, the King.

John is like the prophet Jeremiah, set apart while still in his mother's womb. Even before the two sons were born, John acknowledged the coming of Jesus. We thus learn from Luke's gospel why it was that all Israel came out to hear John's message. He was a prophet of God, set apart with authentic biblical signs: "The Lord's hand was with him." It was the prophet, the last of a long line, who was to announce the birth of Jesus, the Messiah.

Mary's song, like that of Hannah's, sees her promise of a son as a sign that in the birth of this son, God was fulfilling his blessing to Abraham. Zechariah's song sees the birth of John as a sign that God was fulfilling his blessing to Abraham and to David.

Reflection:
Luke's gospel, and its Old Testament Parallels, remind us that God takes barren things and uses them to "yield fruit." God takes something that had no potential and uses it for his glory. In response, people praise God and share the story of what God has done for them. How has God transformed your life? In what ways was your life barren? What fruits are being produced?

Prayer:
God, thank you for taking areas of my life that were barren and using them for your glory. Help me to share with others the story. Give me the courage to acknowledge the ways my life has not always been for your glory. And in the process, may your honor and name be lifted even higher. Amen.

Friday, March 20

Led by The Spirit

Today's Scripture Readings: Luke chapters 3-4

"Jesus, full of the Holy Spirit, left the Jordan and was led by the Spirit into the wilderness," (Luke 4:1)

In chapter 4, Luke once again stresses the role of the Holy Spirit in the work of Jesus: He was "led by the Spirit in the desert." As Israel in the OT was led by the cloud in the wilderness forty years, Jesus was led by the Spirit in the desert where he was then tested by the Devil forty days. The first test came when Jesus had not eaten and was hungry. The Devil said to Jesus, "If you are the Son of God, tell this stone to become bread." When God sent Israel Manna in the desert, it was "to test them and see whether they will follow [his] instructions." Thus, here in Luke's gospel, Jesus answered the Devil's temptation with the lesson Moses himself drew from Israel's test of manna.

Jesus, unlike Israel in the past, did not succumb to the temptation. By means of God's word, he successfully deflected the attacks of the Devil. Luke reminds the reader, however, that though defeated this time, the Devil only made a strategic withdrawal: "he left [Jesus] until the opportune time." Thus the remainder of Jesus' ministry is characterized here as an ongoing battle with the Devil.

Reflection:
How are you led by the Spirit during difficult times? How have you been changed by the Spirit?

Prayer:
Dear Lord, help me see how you are with me not just in the good times but also in the difficult moments of my life. Help me to lean into your grace and mercy. Help me to trust you and learn lessons which will sustain me in my faith for years to come. Amen.

Saturday, March 21

(Self)Righteous

Today's Scripture Readings: Luke chapters 5-6

"I have not come to call the righteous, but sinners to repentance."
(Luke 5:32)

In spite of Jesus' own efforts to carry on a quiet ministry of healing and preaching the good news in the synagogues of Galilee, news of such healings as the leper and the paralytic quickly spread through the region, and Jesus began to attract large crowds. Along with them also came increasing opposition from the leaders of the people.

Jesus was careful to pay respect to and obey the Mosaic Law, but he nevertheless drew sharp attacks from the Pharisees and the teachers of the law. Their opposition, however, only served to further confirm his identity. When the Pharisees asked, "Who can forgive sins but God alone?", Jesus responded with the explanation that it was for precisely this reason that he healed the sick - "that you may know that the Son of Man has authority on earth to forgive sins." His miracles were signs of his identity as the Son of God.

Furthermore, when the Pharisees asked, "Why do you eat and drink with tax collectors and sinners?" Jesus responded by saying it was, in fact, just to these sinners that he had been sent:

"I have not come to call the righteous, but sinners to repentance."
When the Pharisees continued to ask why his disciples did not
fast, it served as an occasion for Jesus to explain his own
relationship with the religious rites and duties of the past: "New
wine must be poured into new wineskins."

Reflection:
It is ironic. Jesus tells the religious leaders that he did not come
to call the righteous, but sinners to repentance. In that moment
the Pharisees missed their opportunity because they viewed
themselves as righteous rather than as sinners in need of
repentance. Yet Paul tells us, quoting the Psalms, "There is no
one righteous, not even one;" (Romans 3:10). Do you view
yourself as righteous or as a sinner in need of repentance? Are
you okay being included with other "tax collectors and sinners?"

Prayer:
Dear Lord, forgive me in my self-righteousness. Amen.

Sunday, March 22

Fidelity

Today's Scripture Readings: Luke chapters 7-8

"Therefore, I tell you, her many sins have been forgiven—as her great love has shown. But whoever has been forgiven little loves little." (Luke 7:47)

Jesus' explanation for his rejection by the religious leaders is disclosed in the act of the sinful woman who washed his feet with her tears, "wiped them with her hair, kissed them and poured perfume on them." The Pharisee who had invited Jesus to his house was unable to understand such devotion to Jesus because, unlike this woman, he had not experienced the depth of forgiveness that this woman had. Besides the twelve apostles, several women also followed Jesus. These, like the woman who washed Jesus' feet, had been forgiven much and had been "cured of evil spirits and diseases." Some also were wealthy. These followers of Jesus were like the seed that landed on the good soil who heard Jesus' word, retained it, and were persevering in producing a crop. They would be richly rewarded and were considered closer than Jesus' own family.

Reflection:
I know that central to my faith is the conviction that I stand in need of unmerited grace from a loving God. However, I also often lose sight of the fact that I stand in need of unmerited grace from

a loving God. It is only in my awareness of my need that I can share with others this unmerited grace from a loving God. Spend time today considering the ways in which you stand in need of unmerited grace from a loving God.

Prayer:
Dear Lord, help me fall more in love with you by becoming more aware of your love for me. Then, in gratitude for your great love, help me to share that love with others. Amen.

Monday, March 23

Lambs Among Wolves

Today's Scripture Readings: Luke chapters 9-10

"Go on your way. See, I am sending you out like lambs into the midst of wolves." (Luke 10:3)

In Luke's gospel, Jesus arrives in Jerusalem in 19:28. There are ten chapters devoted to his journey to Jerusalem. Much in these chapters recounts his teachings to his disciples as well as his deeds.

Luke first recounts that Jesus, on his way to Jerusalem, passed through Samaria. Luke perhaps mentions this to demonstrate the similar pattern of the the spreading of the Gospel in the early church. In Acts, Jesus told the disciples to preach the Gospel "in Jerusalem, and in all Judea and Samaria, and to the ends of the earth." Thus, as Luke presents it, Jesus' ministry has already prepared the way for the Gospel by starting in Galilee and moving to Samaria, Judea, and then to Jerusalem.

As he traveled to Jerusalem, the focus of Jesus' teaching turned to the kingdom of God. In the OT promises, Jerusalem was to be the center of the kingdom. There was a price to pay for those who would enjoy the blessings of God's kingdom. The disciples had to count the cost. Moreover, those who were sent out to proclaim the Gospel of the kingdom had to go as representatives of the King. Jesus thus gave his disciples strict instructions on how to carry out his work. Representatives of God's kingdom must be like lambs among wolves. They are not to seek personal gain, but are to rely on the Lord's provision and accept the help and support of those who serve him. Their message is simple: "The kingdom of God is near you."

Reflection:
In your life are you more like a wolf or a lamb? How would your friends describe you? Your family? Co-workers? Neighbors? Those with whom you disagree?

Prayer:
Holy shepherd, help me to be a lamb rather than a wolf. Protect me. Don't allow me to devour others for my own sake. Amen.

Tuesday, March 24

Worry About Yourself

Today's Scripture Readings: Luke chapters 11-12

"Peter said, 'Lord, are you telling this parable for us or for everyone?'" (Luke 12:41)

With the ever-growing crowd pressing in on him, Jesus began to warn his disciples about the importance of sincerity and honesty before God. Greed and possessions can keep one from the kingdom of God. One must trust in God, not wealth, and live in constant expectation of the coming Son of Man. These exhortations are clearly directed by Luke to the concerns and needs of the early church. Jesus spoke here as one who was looking ahead to a future coming of the Son of Man. That is, he was looking beyond his own rejection in Jerusalem to the future time of his return. This is one of many ways in which Luke's gospel shares the perspective of the early church reflected in the book of Acts.

Luke's perspective of Jesus is highlighted by Peter's question in 12:41: "Lord, are you telling this parable to us, or to everyone?" This question is precisely that of the inquisitive reader of Luke's gospel. Who is Jesus speaking to here? To his disciples or to a much wider audience? His answer further directs his message to those in the early church awaiting the second coming of the Son of Man. The faithful and wise servant, Jesus says, is one whom the master finds doing his will when he returns.

Reflection:
The words of Jesus are meant for those who follow him. Do you live life trusting of God rather than wealth; constantly expecting the coming of the Son of Man? How would your life look different if you really tried to live this way? Would you worry less? Would you enjoy life more? Would it be more stressful?

Prayer:
God, forgive me for all the times I want the words of Jesus to apply to others but not to me. Help me to hear what Christ has to say and allow his words to penetrate my heart. Amen.

Wednesday, March 25

The Banquet

Today's Scripture Readings: Luke chapters 13-14

"When you are invited by someone to a wedding banquet,
do not sit down at the place of honor, in case someone more
distinguished than you has been invited by your host;"
(Luke 14:8)

The kingdom that Jesus offered to Israel represented a break with the ideas of God's kingdom current in his own day. The difference often centered on the meaning of the Sabbath. The religious leaders' understanding of the kingdom was reflected in their anger that Jesus would heal a crippled woman on the Sabbath. Jesus, however, argued that the Sabbath was a time to be set free from bondage. The kingdom of God, rejected in Jesus' own time, would one day fill all the world. Jesus' teaching contains a note of warning to those in Israel: Once the kingdom was rejected, the door would be closed. They would see "Abraham, Isaac and Jacob and all the prophets in the kingdom of God," but they would be cast out. On that day, people would join the kingdom "from east and west and north and south." Luke clearly has in mind here the offer of the kingdom to the Gentiles recounted in Acts. Jesus, however, did not leave Jerusalem without hope. The time would come, he said, when they would again see Jesus coming to Jerusalem in the name of the Lord; the imagery is that of Daniel 7:9-14.

Reflection:
What is your idea and understanding of God's kingdom? Is it reflected in anger? Would you be willing to part with your own ideas of what God's kingdom here on earth should look like?

Prayer:
Dear God, please guide me in the way that leads to peace. Help me to be a humble guest in your kingdom. Amen.

Thursday, March 26

The Rich Man and Lazarus

Today's Scripture Readings: Luke chapters 15-16

"And besides all this, between us and you a great chasm has been set in place, so that those who want to go from here to you cannot, nor can anyone cross over from there to us."
(Luke 16:26)

In Luke 16:16-18, the author shows that Jesus' words must not be understood as canceling the validity of the OT Scriptures: "It is easier for heaven and earth to disappear than for the least stroke of a pen to drop out of the Law." While in the past ("until John") the requirement, even for Gentiles, was to follow the "Law and the Prophets," now "the good news of the kingdom of God is being preached, and everyone is forcing his way into it." As in the early church, Jewish Christians "should not make it difficult for the Gentiles who are turning to God" (Acts 15:19). The Scriptures were to lead sinners to God's kingdom, not to keep them out. If people do not listen to Scripture, "they will not be convinced even if someone rises from the dead." It is significant that in Luke's gospel, even after his own resurrection, Jesus devoted his time to teaching the disciples the Law and the Prophets, and he "opened their minds so they could understand the Scriptures."

Jesus tells the parable of the rich man and Lazarus to teach us what Scripture is about. The rich man, even in his agony, still believes he and his brothers are better than Lazarus. He won't even speak to Lazarus. He asks Abraham to tell Lazarus to bring him water. He then tells Abraham to send Lazarus to warn his brothers. The rich man is so self absorbed he doesn't even realize he has alienated himself. Lazarus has built the chasm and in the process has cut himself off from grace.

Reflection:
When we choose to view others as somehow less than us we begin to separate ourselves from grace. We are no longer people in whom others can find grace. We become people who can no longer receive grace because we do not believe we are in need of grace. We believe we deserve the good we have received and do not even see the grace which comes from God.

Prayer:
Dear Lord, please help me be a person through whom others experience grace. Allow me to see my own need for grace. Enable me to give thanks for the grace I have received. Amen.

Friday, March 27

Humbly Pray

Today's Scripture Readings: Luke chapters 17-18

"But the tax collector stood at a distance. He would not even look up to heaven, but beat his breast and said, 'God, have mercy on me, a sinner.'" (Luke 18:13)

Forgiveness and faith must characterize the life of a disciple (17:1-6); this is the duty of a servant (vv.7-10) and arises out of a grateful heart (vv. 11-19). Though the Pharisees were expecting to see the coming of the kingdom of God in their own day, Jesus warned them that it was already in their midst and they had rejected it (vv.20-21). There was to be a future return of the Son of Man to establish his kingdom, but first it was necessary that Jesus "suffer many things and be rejected by this generation" (v.25). No one knows the time of that coming (vv.26-37). Nevertheless, those who trust in Jesus are to continually offer up prayer that God's kingdom will come (18:1-5). They must not lose heart: "Will not God bring about justice for his chosen ones, who cry out to him day and night?" (v.7). God will "see that they get justice, and quickly" (v.8). The larger question is whether, when he comes, the Son of Man will find anyone continually praying in this way (v.8). Prayer of this sort must be offered in humility. It is characterized by the words of the tax collector: "God, have mercy on me, a sinner" (vv.9-14). One must come to God as a little child (vv.15-17). Such faith is difficult for the rich and the proud, but with God, it is not impossible (vv.18-29).

Reflection:
Are we the tax collectors or the Pharisees? Are we missing, or worse rejecting, the Kingdom of God because it is not what we expect or want it to be? Or are we humbling ourselves before God and acknowledging our own shortcomings? Do we approach God like a little child or are we full of pride?

Prayer:
God, forgive my selfish pride. As this passage of Scripture promises, help me have the faith of a child. Amen.

Saturday, March 28

Whose Authority

Today's Scripture Readings: Luke chapters 19-20

"Tell us by what authority you are doing these things," they said. "Who gave you this authority?" (Luke 20:2)

The King came to Jerusalem, but the kingdom was rejected. Only his disciples recognized him as "the king who comes in the name of the Lord." To the rest "it was hidden." Jesus wept, knowing what great blessings there could have been for Israel and what great judgment lay ahead. As Jesus taught in the temple, events turned quickly and decisively against him.

With the resurrection of Jesus only days away, the Sadducees unwittingly raised a central question (vv.27-44). Jesus assailed the apparent lack of understanding that lay behind their lack of belief in the Resurrection. What they failed to see was that the Scriptures speak of a future that will be altogether different from the past or the present. To understand God's work in Scripture, one cannot merely project the present order into the future. The Resurrection will be a totally different life from present human existence; "they are like the angels." Jesus read Moses and the OT Scriptures quite differently than the leaders at Jerusalem. The Resurrection would not mean a return to the status quo: rather, it would mean a new order of life. Jesus' own resurrection would mark the beginning of that new order.

Reflection:
How does Christ's resurrection impact your understanding of the Scriptures? Does your reading reflect a desire to return to the status quo? How does the resurrection change your understanding of the future? Are you trying to keep things like they are or are you being transformed for a better future?

Prayer:
Dear God, forgive me for when I cling to the present and the status quo. Allow me to be transformed by the resurrection. Allow the resurrection to shape my understanding of what it means to call myself a child of God. Amen.

Sunday, March 29

Jesus' Faithfulness

Today's Scripture Readings: Luke chapters 21-22

"The Lord turned and looked straight at Peter. Then Peter remembered the word the Lord had spoken to him: 'Before the rooster crows today, you will disown me three times.'"
(Luke 22:61)

After being arrested in the garden Jesus was first taken by the chief priests and temple guards into the house of the high priest. Peter, waiting in the courtyard, denied any association with Jesus. When the rooster crowed and Peter had denied him three times, Jesus was close enough to him to be able to cast a knowing glance in his direction, filling him with a sense not only of emptiness of his own vows, "Lord, I am ready to go with you to prison and to death," but also with Jesus' faithfulness, "I have prayed for you, Simon, that your faith may not fail." In this moment, as Jesus casts a look toward Peter, Peter experiences both regret and assurance; loss and hope.

When we think of faith we are often thinking of ourselves and the faith we have in God. Yet in this passage of Scripture it is not Peter's faith that sustains him during this struggle, it is the faith of Christ. It is no surprise that earlier Luke compares the faith of a widow with the faith of the religious leaders (21:1-4). If we are not careful we can fall into the trap of finding in our faith a place of pride.

Reflection:
Spend time today reflecting on your faith. Does your faith lead you to a place of pride or humility?

Prayer:
Dear Lord, help me to not rely on my own faith but to cling to the faith of your Son. Help me to realize that even the faith I have comes from you. Search my heart this day. Where you find pride root it out and replace it with humility. All glory and honor belongs to you. Amen.

Monday, March 30

A Righteous Man

Today's Scripture Readings: Luke chapters 23-24

"Jesus answered him, 'Truly I tell you, today you will be with me in paradise.'" (Luke 23:43)

On the cross, Jesus was surrounded by scoffers. There were three notable exceptions. (1) One of the criminals crucified with Jesus said, "Jesus, remember me when you come into your kingdom" and thus became the first to enjoy the new covenant. (2) The centurion guarding Jesus said, "Surely this was a righteous man." (3) A member of the council that had turned Jesus over to Pilate, Joseph of Arimathea, took the body of Jesus and laid it in his own tomb. Each one of these in his own way understood who Jesus was and openly confessed allegiance to him. The rest of the crowd "beat their breasts and went away," leaving his followers watching "at a distance." Only the women who had been with Jesus followed to see where the body of Jesus was being laid.

Reflection:
It is interesting that each person understood Jesus in their own way. The criminal understood Jesus as a king. The centurion acknowledged Jesus as a righteous man. And Joseph of Arimathea, perhaps finally understood Jesus to be the Messiah. Salvation did not come from a shared understanding. Salvation

does not come from a proper understanding. We do not arrive at salvation through doctrine or theological formulations. Salvation comes from Christ alone. How do you understand Christ? How does your understanding impact your salvation? How does your understanding transform your testimony?

Prayer:
God, forgive me when I inadvertently try to take credit for my own salvation by believing it comes from my proper understanding of who Jesus is and what took place on the cross. Let me find rest, peace, and salvation in your arms alone. Help me to forsake my own understanding. Amen.

Tuesday, March 31

Full of Grace and Truth

Today's Scripture Readings: John chapters 1-2

"The Word became flesh and made his dwelling among us. We have seen his glory, the glory of the one and only Son, who came from the Father, full of grace and truth." (John 1:14)

The gospel of John begins with an introduction to Jesus that goes far beyond the other Gospels. Jesus is the word that was with God before the creation of the world. By him all things were created. This same view of creation is found in the OT book of Proverbs (Pr. 8:22-36). Relying heavily on the images of creation from Genesis, John deliberately blends his images so that he also describes the new creation, i.e., the Gospel and new life that Jesus brought to all humankind. He describes Jesus as the light that shone upon the darkness on the first day of creation. As the darkness was unable to hold back that first light, so the darkness of sin in human hearts could not hold Jesus back. That light gave life to all humankind.

As the Word of God, Jesus became flesh and lived among God's people, Israel. Those who believed in him were given the right to be God's children. Israel had been given a revelation of God's will in the Law of Moses, but they had not seen God. God lived in the tabernacle that Moses built, but his glory was concealed within the Holy of Holies. Jesus revealed God's grace and truth by living among his people. In him they saw God's glory.

Reflection:
As followers of Christ we are called to reflect God's glory in this world in much the same way he did among God's people in Israel. Jesus did this by healing the sick, casting out demons, eating with tax collectors, feeding the hungry, etc. How are you reflecting God in your context? Does it resemble Christ? Is your life full of "grace and truth?"

Prayer:
Dear God, help me to be a reflection of your grace and mercy to those I meet this week. Keep your son, Jesus, in front of my eyes so I may be reminded of the great beauty you have created in this world and be thankful. Amen.

Wednesday, April 1

Redeemer

Today's Scripture Readings: John chapters 3-4

"Jesus answered her, 'If you knew the gift of God and who it is that asks you for a drink, you would have asked him and he would have given you living water.'" (John 4:10)

In the account of the woman at the well, John continues his analysis of Jesus' teaching on the Spirit. The central theme is the "living water" that gives eternal life. The Samaritan woman can only understand Jesus in the context of the well of water from which Jacob drank. But Jesus reminds her that "everyone who drinks this water will be thirsty again."Jesus reveals to the woman that he knows her life and offers her redemption. The author no doubt intends this as an illustration of Jesus' words in the previous chapter: "Whoever lives by the truth comes into the light" and "his deeds will be exposed."

John does not explain what led to the woman's question regarding the dispute between the Jews and the Samaritans about the place of worship. The more important issue is that her question provided a context for raising once again the idea of spiritual worship: "the true worshipers will worship the Father in spirit and in truth." Just as Jacob's well could not quench thirst forever, a physical temple could not provide lasting worship.

The disciples raised a similar question about Jesus' need for physical food, Jesus told them, "I have food to eat that you know nothing about." What food? His disciples were perplexed. "My food," Jesus said, "is to do the will of him who sent me and to finish his work."

John concludes this section with an account of many Samaritans coming to faith in Jesus. Thus Jesus was recognized as more than the Redeemer of Israel: he was "the Savior of the world." This is further demonstrated in the next section where Jesus, a prophet without honor "in his own country," traveled further into Galilee and healed the son of a Gentile official.

Reflection:
As redeemer, what do you need to expose and acknowledge before Christ? How can this be used by God to bring salvation to the world?

Prayer:
Dear Lord, I acknowledge that in order for me to experience your redeeming grace I must turn over the things I believe are hidden. Help me to trust you enough to be vulnerable. Amen.

Thursday, April 2

Son of Man

Today's Scripture Readings: John chapters 5-6

"For just as the Father raises the dead and gives them life, even so the Son gives life to whom he is pleased to give it."
(John 5:21)

In chapter 5 Jesus is back again in Jerusalem. He went to the Pool of Bethesda and there healed a man who had been crippled thirty-eight years. It being the Sabbath day, when the man walked away carrying his own mat, the Jews who saw him were scandalized that he was doing work on the Sabbath. Jesus justified doing work on the Sabbath by appealing to the fact that God, his Father, did not cease work on the Sabbath and "is always at his work to this very day." This answer served only to heighten the anger of these devout Jews against Jesus: "not only was he breaking the Sabbath, but he was even calling God his own Father, making himself equal with God."

Jesus replied to them in a rather lengthy discourse on what it meant to be the Son of God. The context of this discourse is the Son of Man passage in Daniel 7:10-14. In the messianic text of Daniel 7, it is the Son of Man who carries out the task of judgment given to him by the "Ancient of Days." Thus Jesus says, "The Father judges no one, but has entrusted all judgment to the Son." Having identified himself as the Son of Man in Daniel, it was natural for Jesus to turn to the idea of the resurrection from the dead, for the coming of the Son of Man in Daniel is signaled by the resurrection from the dead. Thus Jesus' defense against the accusation that he made himself equal to the Father was his appeal to the Scriptures. He could rightly claim that they "testify" that the Son of Man is equal to the Father. When he completes the work that the Father has given him. The only question that remains is whether those accusing him will accept the authority of the OT. Jesus says, "If you believed Moses, you would believe me, for he wrote about me."

Reflection:
The one that went to the cross for you is the same one who judges you and he has declared you forgiven. How are you using the life given to you by the Son of Man?

Prayer:
Thank you for giving me life. Help me to use it in such a way as to bring you glory and share your grace. Amen.

Friday, April 3

Works

Today's Scripture Readings: John chapters 7-8

> *"You judge by human standards;*
> *I pass judgment on no one." (John 8:15)*

It is interesting to note how John adds a particularly helpful explanation to one of Jesus' discourses. Jesus said, "Whoever believes in me, as the Scripture has said, streams of living water will flow from within him." John adds, "By this he meant the Spirit, whom those who believe in him were later to receive. Up to that time the Spirit had not been given, since Jesus had not yet been glorified." With this explanation, we are enabled to link Jesus' words to the OT's promise of the Spirit (Ezekiel 36:26) as well as to understand the relationship between Jesus' work and the sending of the Spirit at Pentecost in Acts 2. John later records several of Jesus' references to the sending of the Spirit after his departure. In this instance, however, it is John, the author of the book, who makes the comment. Thus we are given an inspired comment on the event at Pentecost after it had happened.

Throughout Jesus' discourses, the opinions remained divided about his identity. Jesus also turned the tables on his opponents and questioned their identity. They claimed to be the children of Abraham, but that would be true only if they did the works that

Abraham did. But if they did the works of the Devil, they ran the risk of becoming children of the Devil.

During this time, the teachers of the law attempted to trap Jesus in a matter of legal interpretation. They brought to him a woman caught in adultery. Their question was whether the stringent requirements of the Mosaic Law should be applied in their day. Jesus' answer was straightforward. Although the law should be carried out, it could not be justly applied. Its administration required a kind of righteousness that did not exist in Israel at that time.

Reflection:
As Christians who live post-resurrection we have received the Holy Spirit and therefore are children of God. But, as we consider the words of Jesus, we can only claim to be the children of God if we do the works of God as demonstrated by Christ. How are you allowing the Spirit to move in your life, helping you do the works of God?

Prayer:
Dear Lord, as I consider the way my life serves as a testimony, please help me to be more like Jesus and less like the teachers of the law. Amen.

Saturday, April 4

His Voice

Today's Scripture Readings: John chapters 9-10

> *"When he has brought out all his own,*
> *he goes on ahead of them, and his sheep follow him*
> *because they know his voice." (John 10:4)*

The failure of his opponents to understand is dramatically portrayed in Jesus' healing the man blind from birth. The meaning John intends for this story is found in Jesus' last words to the Pharisees: "If you were blind, you would not be guilty of sin; but now that you claim you can see, your guilt remains." There are none so blind as those who will not see. Because the blind man knew he was blind, he also knew when he received sight. Those who could see, however, were in danger of confusing their sight with understanding. The blind man could easily draw the conclusion from his healing that Jesus was sent from God: "If this man were not from God, he could do nothing." The Pharisees saw with their eyes but refused to believe. It was to judge such spiritual blindness that Jesus came into the world.

The blind man could not see, but he heard the voice of Jesus and was healed. Jesus is the good shepherd. Like the blind man, his sheep hear his voice and follow him. They do not follow the thief who comes only to steal and destroy. When they hear Jesus and follow him, he gives them life. Though the Pharisees and those listening to these parables do not understand them, the reader has the advantage of having the whole book of John before him. Jesus' parables make much more sense when read from that perspective. It is the prologue to John's gospel that provides the key. Jesus is the one sent from God who came to his own people but who was rejected by them. He was the light of the world that "shines in the darkness, but the darkness has not understood it;" hence, he gives sight to the blind. The light that Jesus gives is life: "In him was life, and that life was the light of men." Though his own rejected him, there were many who would accept him, hence, Jesus has other sheep that will listen to his voice.

Reflection:
The question John seems to be presenting the reader is: Are you trusting in your own "sight" or are you trying to listen for the call of Jesus? Would you recognize his voice?

Prayer:
Dear Lord, help me be aware of my blindness so I come to depend on your voice. Amen.

Holy Week
Palm Sunday, April 5

Lifted Up

Today's Scripture Readings: John chapters 11-12

> *"And I, when I am lifted up from the earth,*
> *will draw all people to myself." (John 12:32)*

There were great crowds in Jerusalem for the celebration of the Passover. They had been looking for Jesus to come and had been alerted by their leaders to report it to them. When Jesus came, however, the crowds rushed into the street, gathering palm branches and shouting "Hosanna! . . . Blessed is the King of Israel." Only after his death and resurrection did his disciples understand; then they saw the whole of his ministry in light of the OT Scriptures.

John, the author of this gospel, keeps the reader fully informed as events happen by supplying the relevant OT texts. Jesus was the King foretold by the OT prophets. He was the Son of David, promised is 2 Samuel 7, and he was the Son of Man, promised in Daniel 7. The fact that the author reminds his readers that the time in which Jesus entered Jerusalem was the time of the Passover is intended to show that Jesus fulfilled the OT; he was the Passover Lamb.

When Gentile Greeks came to Jesus during the time of the Feast, Jesus saw this as a sign that the Son of Man was to be glorified. In Daniel 7, the glorification of the Son of Man is marked by "all peoples, nations and people of every language" coming to worship him." Thus, Jesus later says, "And I, when I am lifted up from the earth, will draw all people to myself."

Reflection:
To be "lifted up from the earth" can be read as a description of the physical act of crucifixion, but it can also be read as a description of Jesus' exaltation in his return to God. The positive effect of Jesus' hour is described in sweeping terms and highlights the universal offer of salvation available in Jesus. It is people's response to this offer that sets limits, not Jesus himself. How are you "lifting" up Jesus? Does it draw people to him?

Prayer:
Dear Lord, help me to live in such a way that I glorify Christ and bring others to him. Amen.

Holy Week
Monday, April 6

Wash One Another's Feet

Today's Scripture Readings: John chapters 13-14

"Now that I, your Lord and Teacher, have washed your feet,
you also should wash one another's feet." (John 13:14)

John understood Jesus' death as the death of Isaiah's Servant of the Lord (Isaiah 52:13-53:12). Thus it was important for him to show that Jesus carried out the role of the Lord's Servant in all respects. This is the central theme of the narrative of Jesus washing the feet of his disciples. The Servant, who gives himself for God's chosen ones, cleanses them thoroughly by his sacrificial death: "Unless I wash you, you have no part with me." The disciples, having already put their faith in Jesus, are clean. Presumably the Servant's death has already cleansed them. They have need only that their feet be washed. They will continue to need their feet washed, and so Jesus sets the example for them: "You also should wash one another's feet." By this he apparently means that the disciples ought to continue to encourage one another in their walk with the Lord and in striving for godliness. Or, as he later explains, "A new command I give you: Love one another. As I have loved you, so you must love one another." As in many of John's narratives, the sense is directed more to the readers of John's gospel than to the disciples within the narratives as such. Thus Jesus tells them,

"You do not realize now what I am doing, but later you will understand."

Reflection:
What does "wash one another's feet" mean to you? How do you live this out? Do you connect this saying of Jesus to his command to love one another?

Prayer:
Dear Lord, help me to look for ways to serve others. Help me to strive to love others even when it is hard. Help me see the goodness in others that you see in me. Amen.

Holy Week
Tuesday, April 7

Waiting

Today's Scripture Readings: John chapters 15-16

> *"I came from the Father and entered the world;*
> *now I am leaving the world and going back to the Father."*
> *(John 16:28)*

John records Jesus' farewell discourse at length (14:1-16:33) and concludes with Jesus' prayer for his disciples. In both the discourse and the prayer, Jesus' words look far beyond the specific needs and concerns of his disciples on the night of his death. They look to the whole of the subsequent history of the church. The background to his words is the teaching of Jesus found throughout the gospel of John. Jesus is the Son of God and the Son of Man. As the Son of God, he had come to fulfill the command of the Father to redeem his chosen people. As the Son of Man, he had come to establish God's kingdom.

The specific issue that the lengthy discourse addresses is the fact that Jesus is about to return to the Father and hence will no longer be physically present with his disciples. They will continue to follow him, however, and wait for his future return. It is this time of waiting and watching that Jesus specifically has in mind throughout the discourse. What are the disciples to do? How are they to carry on his work until he returns?

The key to the meaning of the discourse is given at its conclusion. Jesus said, "I came from the Father and entered the world; now I am leaving the world and going back to the Father." At this point the disciples, who have been quite puzzled throughout the discourse, openly proclaim both their understanding of what Jesus has been saying and their faith in him.

Reflection:
What does it look like to wait for Christ's future return? How are you carrying on his work until Christ returns?

Prayer:
Dear God, don't allow me to sit and wait patiently for your return. Help me to carry on your Son's work until he returns or you call me home. Amen.

Holy Week
Wednesday, April 8

The Spiritual Community

Today's Scripture Readings: John chapter 17

"Holy Father, protect them by the power of your name, the name
you gave me, so that they may be one as we are one."
(John 10:11b)

The one rule of faith that will define the disciples as a believing community will be their love for each other. This love will be the fruit of the Spirit who lives in them. One can easily see that the kind of community that Jesus envisions here is precisely that which unfolds in the book of Acts. This gospel of John presupposes and anticipates the establishment of the church.

In this discourse, Jesus defines more clearly the nature of his community during the time he will be with the Father. It will be the spiritual community of the church. Each individual will be indwelt with the Spirit of God and will have life and bear fruit as a branch of a vine. It is this form of spiritual life that Jesus had spoken about to the Samaritan woman: "The true worshipers will worship the Father in spirit and truth." It was this that Jesus spoke of on the day of the feast when he said, "Whoever believes in me, as the Scripture has said, streams of living water will flow from within him" - to which John explained, "By this he meant the Spirit, whom those who believed in him were later to receive." It is this Spirit which binds us together and makes us one as the Father and Son are one.

Reflection:
Our ability to have life and bear fruit as a spiritual community is dependent on our ability to love each other. This is the one thing that Jesus says is evidence of our discipleship. All of this is the fruit of the Spirit who lives within us. How well are we loving one another? How well are you loving others in your community of faith?

Prayer:
Dear Lord, help me love others as you love me. Help me to love others even when they make it difficult. Help me to remember that I am sometimes difficult to love. Amen.

Holy Week
Maundy Thursday, April 9

I Am Not

Today's Scripture Readings: John chapter 18

*"You aren't one of this man's disciples too, are you?" she asked
Peter. He replied, "I am not." (John 18:17)*

John 18:13-27, similar to 18:1-12, presents the reader with two
contrasting images. One is the image of Jesus, who willingly
offers himself to those who come to arrest him and boldy
answers those who interrogate him. The other is the image of
Jesus' disciples who betray and deny the one who so freely gives
his life for them. The other characters in these scenes, the
Roman soldiers, the temple police, even Annas and Caiaphas,
merely provide the background against which this drama
between Jesus and his own is acted out.

Judas' betrayal of Jesus is the more dramatic action, but Peter's
denial may be the most haunting. Judas' betrayal bears
testimony to the power of evil and so is a reminder of the cosmic
drama that is acted out in Jesus' life and death. Peter's denials
are not placed on such a grand stage, however. Instead, Peter's
denials occupy that gray area, marked not by outright betrayal,
but by the compromise and acquiescence to personal
expediency, self-protection, and fear.

Peter's denials are even more painful and haunting when they are placed in their wider context in the Gospel narrative. At the farewell dinner, Jesus acted out his love for his disciples in the foot washing, addressing Peter individually about his share in Jesus' life. In the farewell discourse, Jesus reassured his disciples about his abiding presence with them and declared his love for them. In the garden and in front of Annas, he showed he would lay down his life for them. Yet, with the farewell address words of Jesus still echoing in his ears, Peter cannot even publicly claim his place as Jesus' disciple.

Reflection:
As we draw near to Easter take time today to consider how you have denied Jesus. Ask yourself the question, "How have I put myself before Christ?"

Prayer:
Dear Lord, forgive me for those moments when I fail to respond to the love you have shown me because I am afraid and put my own concerns first. Amen.

Holy Week
Good Friday, April 10

It Is Finished

Today's Scripture Readings: John chapter 19

"When Jesus had received the wine, he said, 'It is finished.' Then he bowed his head and gave up his spirit." (John 19:30)

John recounts the crucifixion of Jesus in such a way that its fulfillment of OT prophecies is highlighted. Particularly important to John is the identification of Jesus as the King of the Jews. Thus in the title given to Jesus at his death, he was recognized as the Davidic King, the Messiah, and the Son of Man who received the kingdom. More importantly, it was a Gentile Roman official who called him "King of the Jews," just as in the book of Daniel, it is the Gentile nations who acknowledge the Son of Man as King of the Jews.

In keeping with John's emphasis on the work that Jesus was sent into the world to do, the final words of Jesus he records are simply "It is finished." Jesus had completed the work of the Father. John's focus on the fact that the Roman guards did not break Jesus' legs but instead pierced his side is linked to his desire to show that even in the smallest details, the fulfillment of OT prophecies give witness to Jesus as the Messiah.

In his account of the burial of Jesus, John shows that two "secret" Jewish believers, Joseph of Aramathea and Nicodemus, openly acknowledged their faith in Jesus. There may be a suggestion here that many more such believers were to be found among even the leaders of the people.

Reflection:
At first, it appears that John may be suggesting the Jewish leaders have missed out on the coming of their own Messiah and therefore they have forfeited their inheritance to the Gentiles. Yet, the arrival of Joseph of Aramathea and Nicodemus suggests it is never too late. Even in Jesus' final words, "It is finished" we see that God is just getting started. Is there someone you have given up on? Is it you? What can you do to reach out to them?

Prayer:
Dear Lord, help me not to give up on friends, family, and even myself. May I find strength in your unending love and faithfulness. Amen.

Holy Week
Saturday, April 11

Belief Without Understanding

Today's Scripture Readings: John chapter 20

"He saw and believed. (They still did not understand from Scripture that Jesus had to rise from the dead.)" (John 20:8b-9)

The empty tomb narratives counter the sentimental notions of the resurrection and reunion with Jesus. Peter and the beloved disciple are given nothing but the evidence of an empty tomb. The effect of that evidence on Peter is not stated in the text, but its impact on the beloved disciple is clear, "he saw and believed." No angelic announcement accompanies the glimpse into the empty tomb, no reassuring words that Jesus has risen, that he has gone before them. There is only the stark emptiness of the tomb and the telltale presence of Jesus' abandoned burial clothes; yet the beloved disciple believes.

How can the evidence of an empty tomb lead to faith? The beloved disciple believed because he already believed. That is, because the beloved disciple believed in Jesus and the trustworthiness of his promises about himself and God. When he saw the empty tomb, he knew what it signaled: that Jesus conquered death. The beloved disciple did not know what form Jesus' conquest of death had taken; he did not know how Jesus' conquest of death would be manifested among the living; he did not even know how to speak about what he saw in the tomb. All he knew was what the burial clothes told him: that Jesus had defeated death.

In John 20:3-10, the author of John presents the reader with a character who embodies the faith, who does not "judge by appearances," but "with right judgment" (7:25). It is important that the contemporary Christian community heeds this story and lingers with the witness of the empty tomb before moving to stories of the risen Jesus.

Reflection:
Spend today, the day before Easter, contemplating the empty tomb. What evidence do you require to have faith? Is your faith dependent on your understanding? Can you follow Christ without being able to answer the questions that arise as a result of the empty tomb?

Prayer:
Dear Lord, help me to follow in the footsteps of the beloved disciple. Help me believe even as I stare into the emptiness of a tomb. Amen.

Easter
Sunday, April 12

Feed My Lambs

Today's Scripture Readings: John chapter 21

"When they had finished eating, Jesus said to Simon Peter, 'Simon, son of John, do you truly love me more than these?' 'Yes, Lord,' he said, 'You know that I love you.' Jesus said, 'Feed my lambs.'" (John 21:15)

At the conclusion of this gospel, John summarizes his purpose in writing. He has given the reader an account of the signs and miracles that Jesus did, proving that Jesus is the Christ, the Son of God. By believing in Jesus, life is offered in his name. Thus, in the epilogue of this book, John returns to the theme of life in Christ that was the focus of the prologue: "In him was life, and that life was the light of humankind. . . to all who received him, to those who believed in his name, he gave the right to become children of God" (1:4, 12).

The account of the third and last appearance of Jesus in Galilee presents a picture of the future ministry of the disciples as fishers of people. The meaning John intends is transparent. When the disciples follow the words of Jesus, they will make many disciples. John clearly intends his gospel to be a guide to the words of Jesus. Jesus had said, "I, when I am lifted up from the earth, will draw all people to myself" (12:32). By means of this book, the message of Jesus will be heard and received by many.

Jesus' final instructions to the disciples is to care for his growing number of disciples: "Feed my lambs" (21:17). Jesus' first words to his disciples was, "Follow me" (1:43); that was also his last (21:19).

Reflection:
We often think about being "fed" by going to church, reading our Bibles, participating in Sunday School, going on mission trips . . . But in the end, Jesus tells Peter to "Feed my lambs." The first call of discipleship is to follow Jesus, but to follow Jesus also means caring for others who follow Jesus. You have been fed. How are you "feeding" Christ's lambs?

Prayer:
Dear God, today we celebrate the resurrection of your son, Jesus. Help me to see that this was not just for me but for all. Give me the courage and strength to not only receive but to share the grace you so freely give. Amen.

Made in the USA
Coppell, TX
11 February 2020

15711312R00067